A NEW KIND OF BLEAK

Journeys Through Urban Britain

OWEN HATHERLEY

VERSO
London • New York

This paperback edition first published by Verso 2013
First published in by Verso 2012
© Owen Hatherley 2012, 2013

1 3 5 7 9 10 8 6 4 2

Verso
UK: 6 Meard Street, London W1F 0EG
US: 20 Jay Street, Suite 1010, Brooklyn, NY 11201
www.versobooks.com

Verso is the imprint of New Left Books

ISBN-13: 978-1-78168-075-9

British Library Cataloguing in Publication Data
A catalogue record for this book is available from the British Library

Library of Congress Cataloging-in-Publication Data
A catalog record for this book is available from the Library of Congress

Typeset in Fournier by MJ Gavan, Truro, Cornwall
Printed and bound by CPI Group (UK) Ltd, Croydon, CR0 4YY

...We wanted something new, and we
Would sacrifice most anything
(Well, decorum *definitely)*
To get our gawky, sky-jostling
Ruck with nature set in knifey
Portland stone. Of course, I know
Time hasn't widened out the way
We reckoned all those years ago.
You plan for that, allow for that.
I know the building might have housed
The odd careerist democrat
Or two, and yes, we missed
Our chance to make a truly ideal
Hive, a fair organic whole.
That too was calculable.
Facts played their usual role.
What niggles like a buzzing clock
Are certain Belgian sightseers,
How they so leisurely mock
Our bid to level with the stars,
How smiling artisans can stare
Me dead in the eye, ecstatically
Perplexed when I say future.
We wanted something new, you see.

— Alex Niven

Contents

by something more square-bourgeois – Bennetts' new Jubilee Library, and the several blocks around it. The Library itself is a surprisingly confident building, especially for a PFI and Design and Build contract, something which usually guarantees shoddiness. Its elegance is almost entirely down to neat proportions and the decision to clad much of it in deep blue glazed tiles, a subtle nod to one of the city's Victorian materials, which fits the general raffishness very nicely. Somewhat less successful is the obligatory thwacking big atrium, which is visible through a blue glass façade soiled by the city's anti-social seagulls. The blocks around, housing the usual middle-class chains – Wagamama, etc – are inoffensive, if bland, so it's the offsetting that offends: the notion that a library must be justified by lots of surrounding retail, something that long pre-dates the current war on the public sector. The entrance to PizzaExpress is far more prominent than that of the Library itself.

Fashionable Brighton is not nearly as interesting as it thinks it is. In fact, the element of the city that really convinces, that saves it from completely irredeemable smugness, is the tourists' seafront promenade, and the dense fringe of grandiose houses and apartments along it. One route takes you past irksome retail, old (the twee maze of The Lanes, where it is acceptable to call a shop 'Pretty Eccentric') and new (CZWG's Black Lion Street, a rather imaginative, angular infill building which unfortunately houses a Jamie Oliver restaurant). Then you get to this sweeping vista, somewhere between a Regency utopia and a Brutalist Miami, defined most magnificently by a feeling of space and air without parallel in the UK, with a wide boulevard, open lawns, and the Channel spread out before you. It's glorious, and that glory is given particular pathos by the ruins of the West Pier, a haunting reminder of the city's persistent hint of the sinister. Giant towers are planned and seemingly shelved at each end of this imposing ensemble – a monster hotel by Wilkinson Eyre to the west, an observation tower by Marks Barfield to the east. The latter was supposed to replace the ruins of the West Pier with a huge, 1960s TV Tower-like contraption. No construction can be seen, but the hoardings promising various delights are still there, now considerably worn.

The Apotheosis of the Luxury Flat

Celebrity architectural scribbler Frank Gehry had a scheme in the Planning Department at Hove for some years during the boom. It entailed one small architectural element by the man himself, twisty and aluminium-clad to make sure you knew who it was; that was then hemmed in, to make it profitable, by several very dense and very bland blocks of luxury flats. It is now not so much shelved as permanently cancelled, although that's no great tragedy, as the scheme bore about as much relation to Gehry's best work as Walter Gropius's Playboy Club in Park Lane did to the Dessau Bauhaus. As it is, modernism in the centre of Brighton is represented by some still controversial structures. One scheme surely due some critical rehabilitation is the Brighton Centre and the accompanying Odeon, designed by Russell Diplock Associates. Both sit at the point where Brutalism and futurist kitsch meet, and are all the better for it, with the Odeon's expressionistic roofline a particular thrill. Even more hated by custodians of Brighton are the several Richard Seifert schemes that crowd behind Alfred Waterhouse's aggressively red, late-Victorian Hotel Metropole and the fussy redesign that the IRA inadvertently facilitated for the Grand. There is one unforgivable element to this complex, where Seifert's additions extend to sawing off Waterhouse's skyline, replacing it in the clumsiest, lamest manner possible with flat extra floors – but the irregular grids of the Seifert towers themselves are very smart, both up close and from a distance, adding a metropolitan skyline drama which, along with the council high-rises in the east of the city, stops the townscape from becoming a mildly more boho seaside version of Bath.

The other major modernist scheme creates a demarcation between Brighton and Hove, both in terms of scale and style, but it's of far more than local significance. Wells Coates's 1936 Embassy Court, recently and thoroughly restored, follows on the experiments of his Isokon housing block in London. The latter, a small development in Hampstead, was an attempt to recreate Central European Modernist communal living, largely inhabited by Weimar exiles. Embassy Court expands the concept into a huge, physically powerful block. It might have been built as serviced flats for light entertainers, but it's clear here how much Coates was indebted to Constructivism, especially Moisei Ginzburg's Narkomfin Communal House in Moscow. The seaside front is clean, curved and classic, but prowl round the corner and the building's circulation is on spectacular display, with strongly, bulgingly modelled access decks and staircases, rendered in thick cream, so lush that you feel you could eat them – it supports Manfredo Tafuri's one-time description of Coates as a 'proto-Brutalist'. While chromatically it is of a piece with Regency Hove, the architectural ideas are entirely those of far-left inter-war Europe; as apparently are too the very small *existenzminimum* proportions of the flats inside. What was originally intended as an imagine-no-possessions gesture is reimagined as the no-frills bed for the night of a seedy seaside assignation. In the combination of metropolitanism, grand architectural ambitions and general seediness, Embassy Court is all the best things about Brighton and Hove in one concrete structure. It's one of the most remarkable blocks of flats in the country, among several more prosaic apartment blocks of the same era in Hove.

First you pass through Brunswick Town, which is as complete an expression of Regency luxury aesthetics as Embassy Court is of the '30s, an often breathtaking collection of crescents and squares. Looking at the way the bow-windowed terraces sweep down the hills to the sea, it's hard not to sense that here there was a real seriousness about high-design, high-density living combining with hierarchy, profit-making and speculation. It is what William Cobbett would have considered an emanation of the Wen, an export of London into the Sussex countryside (then just a stroll away), overbearing, prissy, pretentiously modish. In the urban island that we live in now, rather than the rural one Cobbett saw destroyed, it is utterly exemplary. Brunswick Town and its related developments were evidently the Urban Renaissance of their day, and they were certainly as shabby – the classical façades are a mere front, with seediness always strongly visible round the back. The difference between these and the speculations two centuries thence is that these are immeasurably more confident and proud in architectonic execution. Looking at the central crescents

of the development, spiralling wildly uphill, they seem more modern than ever – the dozens of bays are as rhythmic and repetitive as anything designed in the 1960s. What they make clear is just how seriously these designers, stock-jobbers and speculators took the architectural problem of building metropolitan architecture at a very high density and on a very large scale. They didn't get round it by offsetting the mass with gestures of irregularity, instead they accentuated it, with a dominant rationalist sweep that encompasses rather than differentiates. The result, in a city of self-proclaimed individualists, is that it feels as much a piece of deferred collective housing as does Embassy Court.

Go up the hill a bit from here, and you find much more of this luxury high-density housing, all of it exceptionally seductive. Bethnal Green was once described as a living museum of working-class housing. If so, then Hove is a living museum of the luxury flat. Every permutation is on show. The Jeeves and Wooster neo-Georgian of Wick Hall, now a Buddhist Centre ('Meditate in Brighton', it suggests – a new, more pious approach to self-help); the Crittall Windows and wave motifs of Furze Court, with additional Bupa centre. Eric Lyons's typically elegant Span Development at Park Gate. Gwydyr Mansions, a neo-Flemish tenement block which, at the back, shows a weird conjunction of rectitude (neatly Georgian windows) and accidental modernism (stark concrete access balconies). At St Anne's Court and Beresford Court, there are especially outré combinations of traditionalism and '30s metropolitan display, where odd Byzantine turrets, Tudor timbering and Georgian brickwork meet De Stijl doorways and futurist-styled stained glass. St Anne's Court has a blue plaque informing us that Lord Alfred Douglas once lived here.

The newer blocks of flats make exactly the same move, on exactly the same low-to-mid-rise scale, for exactly the same kind of clientele – Hove's sleepy and/or elderly population, and the usual trickle of ex-Londoners – but are glaringly clumsy and poorly executed by comparison. Take Landsdowne Court, with its blocky red terracotta cladding and strikingly cheap-looking balconies – it could be in any number of less favoured, less wealthy towns. The blocks next to Beresford Court are especially alarming – here, perhaps as some consequence of the salty winds coming in off the sea, the wood panelling has deteriorated so rapidly that it looks burnt. In fact, it looks like the boarding councils use to deter squatting. It's all indicative of one of the stranger things for which the last thirty years can be indicted – that so often, even the luxury housing was poor. It seems to sum up a few truths about this attractive if impressively hypocritical city. At least from the elevated points of Hove you can walk down to the seafront, take in those winds and that space, and pretend that everything's going to be alright.

Genteel Brutalism

If you take another approach to Hove, the effect is quite different from Brunswick Town's showpiece drama. If you walk along the seafront, well into Hove's less populous, less festive half of the water, then you suddenly find the line of grand hotels being broken by several immense blocks of modern flats. This is Grand Avenue, named in an earlier era. If this were practically anywhere else in the country, save perhaps for the Royal Borough of Kensington and Chelsea, a place looking like Grand Avenue would be branded a sink estate, the brick would be discoloured and the concrete would be cancerous, and it would be either massively overcrowded or recently 'decanted'. Here, it appears that the metropolitan quiet and high-density isolation of high-rise living signifies luxury. I don't exaggerate. On the west side are the three identical, serried blocks of Warnham Court, concrete with brick infill, a completely generic 1960s design, where the major difference is partly one of clientele, partly one of density, as they don't even have the surrounding greenery that usually accompanies blocks of this sort in a real council estate. The biggest of them all, the overbearingly bulky Coombe Lea, would surely be considered a horror block, an eyesore, anywhere but a place this genteel. For all that, the look of cheapness should not be overstated; they're really no more or less cheap or jerry-built than the terracotta guest houses whose space they barge into. On the other side of the central reservation, the blocks have more pretensions – art deco mouldings, expressive balconies, nice moderne typography, a hint of Brightons past and the skulduggery that may have taken place in them. This little cluster of high-rise, high-density modernism is centred around a statue of Queen Victoria, which can't help but feel apt.

Walk a little further on from here, past some lost Arts and Crafts semis and rather more decorative tenements, and you get to Hove Town Hall, a wild-eyed vindication of 1960s modernity in the most unlikely place. Designed by Wells-Thorpe and Partners in 1970, it is not a building that is remotely interested in keeping up appearances. Put together in a decade when there were serious thoughts about demolishing large swathes of Regency Brighton and Hove, and when skyscrapers started appearing just behind the Grand Hotels, it abandons any thought of contiguous urbanism with its Victorian surroundings in favour of a supreme, isolated and grandiose object-building. As a piece of architecture it is a monstrously successful achievement; it doesn't need a context, it creates its own. The houses and flats around are forced to pay tribute. Yet it doesn't register its centrality through height, but through compaction.

The complex is asymmetrically arranged, with a corner clock tower and wings, detailed in a thickly ribbed grey concrete, mostly kept in very good condition. There is a lot of glass, but not in the contemporary 'transparent' manner – quite the reverse, in fact, with the material smoked into a mean, moody nicotine brown, with every Sussex bureaucrat able to play at starring in *All The President's Men*. Each floor is slightly boxed-out, so that the complex appears as several intersecting black and grey ziggurats. The interiors, also, have a compulsive, Cold War intensity, with expensive materials and sharply modern patterns running through the ceremonial spaces. At one corner, Hove's coat of arms is embossed into the concrete, meticulously detailed in red, blue and shimmering gold mosaic. The service areas round the back, with their glass walkways and deep concrete curves, are worth a wander just in themselves. The only persistent question is: how on earth did this get built here, by these people? When and how did post-war Conservative councillors in Sussex seaside towns acquire a taste for the avant-garde? The question loses some of its edge when one remembers that the Tory Party of Edward Heath was practically the SWP by contemporary standards, but the point remains. Were they just hoodwinked by clever architects, or was Brighton and Hove seriously trying to become the seaside town of the future?

The Seedy Side

If so, they were quickly defeated by conservationists, particularly after the 'damage' done to the seaside skyline by the council towers in the east and Seifert's cluster round the Hotel Metropole. Obviously on some level this was all to the good – no amount of Hove Town Halls could justify the demolition of Brunswick Town – but conservationism does sound like conservatism for more than aural reasons. In a recent and very informative architectural guide to Brighton and Hove, it is claimed that the siting of Brighton's more, shall we say, *demotic* seaside attractions on the 'usefully remote' main pier has the effect of not lowering the tone too much, of keeping all that flashy prole spectacle at a safe distance from the raffish and delicate promenade frontage. Aside from the objectionable tone of such a description, this is very much how the Pier relates to the rest of the city; a reservation of the sort of tackiness you'd usually go to Southend, Bournemouth or Blackpool to experience. For these reasons it is worth visiting, although not just for these reasons.

If I describe Brighton sneeringly, that is not at all the intention, more something that creeps in almost against my will – an inability not to be a little chippy about the place, along with a reluctance to condemn it entirely. In my early twenties, I knew this place better than anywhere but London and my home town, and always had very conflicted feelings about it. I come from the south coast's largest city (it's nice to find a superlative for it), thirty or so miles westwards, a working city with none of the urbane sophistication of Brighton and Hove, although of a similar size and in a similar part of the country. Coming from such a place, Brighton was both fascinating and irritating – irritating because it seemed to have absolutely no idea of just how bloody lucky it was. Everybody I knew in Brighton was in a band. Every last one of them. Some weren't when I met them, but they soon succumbed. Some of those bands went on to have the odd NME cover, some of them are Big in Japan, some just played a handful of gigs, but the point wasn't whether they were good or not. The point was that they all appeared to think it was completely natural and normal that they would spend their lives writing songs, recording, and continually bumping into each other outside the Komedia or in the awe-inspiring antiquarian hangar of Snooper's Paradise in North Laine; and yet they seldom ran out of money. This, for them, was just the way things were; the creative class are not much better at thinking outside their circumstances than any other section of the bourgeoisie. For me, pop culture was something transformative, unexpected – the sheer strangeness of finding the hyper-intellectual, wildly pretentious world of the music press in your local Spar was a door to another world, whereas for them it was something familiar to the point of being boring. The non-musical aspects were of no import. The songs speak for themselves. The music's the thing. I found all that hard to forgive, although the tide of history was evidently with them. My younger brother, seduced in his own way, went as far as moving here, and within months despised the place with a passion. 'Fucking Toytown', was his neatest way of describing his problem with

it. But seductive is really exactly what it is – a quick visit to
Snooper's Paradise brings it all back with great intensity. A stall
full of '60s New Left paperbacks, Raymond Williams, Wilhelm
Reich and Stokely Carmichael; racks upon racks of brightly coloured artificial fabrics, giving your fingers a static electric tingle;
box after box of worn, pungent vinyl; the SF-boy manna of an
entire Dr Who section. Only the smell of the industrial-strength
hydroponics is absent.

The significance of the above is that I found myself inadvertently retracing my way to the house in Kemptown where I used
to outstay the welcome of a friend's parents. It is, coincidentally,
a great route for watching elegant Brighton decompose in a short
space and time. Walk north and east from the Pier, past the only
new church in this book (almost amusingly bad, a poky little
addition to the ground floor of a shoddy block of flats), and you
arrive at the big bad Brighton tower blocks. Some of them really
are impressive in their out-of-scale pride and confidence, their
dimensions overwhelming smaller neighbours. But this is still
Brighton, and so those neighbours are often so strange as to make
the juxtaposition a genuinely surrealist one; a little toy castle lurks
alongside twenty storeys, doubled around a glass stair tower, in
black and brown concrete. Further uphill, you find half-timbered

Edwardian townhouses overlooked by serried stock-brick blocks, and these must command views so magnificent that, a generation or two after lifelong council-house tenure is abolished, they will surely be a preserve of the exceedingly rich. At the corner of the street is what looks like a cross between a bunker and the Rhino House at London Zoo, its concrete moulded in subtle, shallow curves. In the places where Brighton stops being affluent, it doesn't stop being Brighton, and that is one of the better things about the city.

That said, at this distance I can't possibly understand why such enthusiasts for mind-altering substances as those I knew in Brighton were so seldom attracted to the Pier. Ideally, Brighton Pier needs to be visited at night, for the full psychotropic effect of its neon pulsations to be experienced. At first, as you enter, it's a fairly normal bit of kiss-me-quick neo-Victoriana, with nostalgic iconography highlighting the strange fact that at the seaside, there are only two real eras of significance – a prurient, repressed Victorian age, and a prurient, repressed 1950s. That's not why you should come here if you're interested in architecture. The reason why is the dodgems, which has a space frame roof trimmed in pink and purple tubes of neon. Or the Waltzer,

where a yellow-orange-red sunburst sits atop the metal construction holding up the tilted cars. Or 'Scream', of which the caption says 'It's Extreme'. Or the Crazy Mouse, a children's board game reproduced in three dimensions and built twenty feet high. I'm not suggesting that you actually go on any of these rides, unless you want to. Instead, more of a question: who dares deny that in the crackling electricity of all this, its current of vivid pleasure, there's something far more urban and metropolitan than the most well-appointed of Regency Crescents? And something more *other* than the self-conscious 'alternative'?

Chapter Eight

Croydon: Zone 5 Strategy

Super-Dormitory

After the collapse of the Urban Renaissance, the suburbs are back, that much is clear. That preceded the election of the Tory–Whig government. Boris Johnson's 'Zone 5 Strategy' proved again how successful a politician can be by appealing to the Free-Born Englishman's age-old right to drive at four miles an hour rather than taking a bus, and since then the Party of government has explicitly favoured suburban, South East England, especially as the North becomes more hostile to it. Croydon, as the largest single area in Surrey and the largest Outer London borough, may be regarded as a fairly representative slice of the London/Home Counties grey area that has been a Conservative bastion for over a century, and that effectively governs the UK. It can serve here, in theory, as a typical exemplar of Home Counties Suburbia, in the same place as, say, Guildford, Woking, Watford, High Wycombe; areas designed as dormitories for City clerks, that have flourished to the point where they generate their own inward pull, and then their own peripherally located business parks, malls and factories. But why is it, then, that the first impression a stranger might have of central Croydon is that of a teeming, multicultural, independent provincial city? Why does the London Borough of Croydon so much want to be a City itself? And what can we learn about what a 'suburb' really is from this place?

Croydon regularly bids to receive the official title of 'City', and if it ever gets to fulfil its long-stated wish to drop the 'sub' from its 'urban', this quintessential commuter suburb will become a city of above average size, with roughly the extent and population of, say, Coventry or Hull. Croydon already has its own rapid transport system and its own rather particular pattern of urbanism, ahead of several official British cities. Many in South East England will be familiar with the strange sight that hits you when leaving East Croydon station. What with the trams and high-rises, you could believe you were in a wealthy West German industrial city – somewhere that is entirely confident about its own modernity, that willingly inhabited the late twentieth century without looking over its shoulder. The trams, too, are an unexpected joy, taking you from New Addington to Wimbledon, should you require such a service, while threading their lines above eye level. The contrast with both the average London suburb and the average English city is sharp indeed, until you walk around a little. Then the landscape starts to become familiar, and fast.

What you find on investigation is that Croydon is very English indeed: a result of the subjugation of planning to commerce. In short, in the 1960s an ambitious council offered businesses cheap office space, close to London, if they would fund infrastructural improvements. Within an astonishingly short time, a burb was transformed into a minor metropolis of skyscrapers, underpasses and flyovers; the trams would come rather later, but have a similarly metropolitan air. Since then the place has been the butt of numerous jokes. 'Mini-Manhattan', as if trying to be like New York was somehow less interesting than being like Surbiton. Croydon had, and has, ideas above its station, and for that it's hard not to warm to it. Yet the problem with the place quite quickly becomes apparent. The dashing appearance from a distance gives way to a messy, chaotic reality, contrived in the good old, ad hoc, throw-everything-in-the-air-and-see-where-it-lands style so beloved of England.

Mini-Manhattan Revisited

In its ethos, the erstwhile Croydon of the Future resembles the Enterprise Zones of the 1980s. The towers are constructed at random, oblivious to one another, allowed to go as high in any

place as the developers wanted. For that, it is hardly a paragon of social democratic urbanism, but in aesthetic it's a 1960s living museum, left remarkably intact. A complete post-war skyline, accompanied only by a mere couple of recladdings, and only two completed post-1970s towers – an office block and an apartment block. Neither of these is of the slightest architectural note, though skyscrapers by Norman Foster and Make were planned before the crash, and a barcode façade can slowly be seen creeping up a concrete core near West Croydon station. As it stands, much of what you can see is mosaic, concrete and glass in the English corporate modernist manner. Accordingly, central Croydon has an accidental uniqueness: things obliterated elsewhere persist here. It's strictly for the enthusiast – there's a lot of period charm and plenty of places where you can re-enact your own personal kitchen-sink film, but not much in terms of real architectural quality. Richard Seifert's fabulous hexagonal NLA Tower, probably that firm's finest essay in tectonic corporate branding, along with Centre Point and NatWest, is justifiably regarded as Mini-Manhattan's Empire State, the block that features on the promotional literature. It was recently repainted and restored, but there's little else that shows any spark. The pleasure instead is in seeing the recent past's generic, everyday architecture in an unusual state of completeness and survival.

A walk around this suburban metropolis would take in the once chic, now shabby tapering tower the council built for their own offices, which nicely complements their earlier, enjoyably debased Victorian halls; a couple of sub-Seifert cubist experiments; a jollily Festival of Britain Travelodge in brick and zigzag render; Hilberseimer-style Zeilenbau blocks stepping along in enfilade wherever a developer could get a big enough plot; and in the distance, the chimneys of a disused power station ornamenting a giant IKEA. The problem, or for the dedicated flâneur, the fun, is in how it interacts with the suburb all around, or rather how it doesn't. Arrangements are totally random – a row of artisans' terraces with skyscrapers behind, would-be secluded Tudorbethan facing giant high-rises, the sound of birdsong vying with an endless rumble of traffic. Sometimes the place seems to be mocking itself, as when a churchyard meets a concrete subway you find the sign: 'OLD TOWN CONSERVATION AREA'. In fact, there's a lot of pre-Victorian, never mind pre-1960s remnants in among the towers, if you know where to find them – vestiges of Croydon's unlikely former existence as a religious centre. The Victorian buildings suggest a place that already considered itself a cut above the average suburb – large-scale department stores that belie the ability to get to Selfridges in twenty-five minutes from East Croydon station.

In its sense of chaos and drama, Croydon seems to have rather little in common with the typology of the commuter dormitory, but appears instead as a slice of Inner London on the lam. One of the more thrilling, and telling, moments is at the back-end of the mini-metropolis, where the office-block landscape suddenly meets market stalls, butchers' shops and caffs, while a black steel walkway stretches across to connect it to a block of yuppie flats. In that tension is encapsulated what makes central Croydon feel as much a part of London proper as Peckham or Tottenham, albeit much more distant from the centre. The accidental ensemble creates an acutely surreal urban experience, taking the capital's pre-existing aptitude for juxtaposition and amplifying it. The most memorable part of it all, comfortingly but atypically, is an enclave of public space, the St George's Walk arcade, which emerges from behind the drab Nestlé Tower. Part is open to the air, part is shell-roofed, with the rest propped up by mosaic-clad pilotis. It's elegant, but it doesn't manage to meaningfully connect with anything else. The place is divided and carved up, very literally. A walk from East Croydon to West Croydon railway stations initially takes you through a Business Improvement District, one of those privately owned, privately patrolled 'solutions' for urban management – which in this case means clean streets and a large quantity of CCTV cameras. It ends remarkably suddenly, just by West Croydon station, where dirt, rubbish and relatively 'unsightly' hoardings and shop signs take over, and the mood is fractious. Waiting for a bus here provides a front-line seat for crisis, with vicious arguments between shoppers seemingly treated as normal.

'Oi, Cleanshirt!'

The residential Croydon that lies outside the Business Improvement District is somewhat uncharted. Near the NLA tower is some very low-density, lush suburbia, much of it turned into consultancies, dentists' offices and other commercial uses. One large Arts and Crafts house in the shadow of the skyscrapers purports to be the Croydon and Bromley School of Philosophy, which charges for courses in 'practical philosophy'. A rare new tower, a metal-clad tube of zero merit, is just adjacent. Residential towers are massively outnumbered by the offices nearby, but there's some worth noting. The council estates that lurk just past the flyover have a couple of surprises, such as the Festival of Britain stylings of the Cromwell Tower, as worn and unclad as the centre's office blocks. The most notable block, however, is Zodiac House, which fans of the sitcom *Peep Show* will be familiar with. It's an enjoyable piece of 1960s kitsch, with bronze zodiac signs placed upon the ground-floor podium, which houses mostly shops that evidently went to seed a very long time ago; the flats above are well-detailed in concrete and brick, with very large windows, and look rather chic, despite the mess all around. It is apt enough as a location, given that *Peep Show* has been one of the few programmes on television in recent years to dare look twenty-first-century London in the eye, with its grim office jobs, its class divisions, its trust-funded layabouts, its compulsory business bullshit, its air of suppressed hopelessness covered with desperate hedonism. With the possible exception of the trust funds, all of these seem present and correct here.

So Croydon seems, at first, nothing like the kempt and leafy commuter enclave that a suburb is supposed to be. First it's a Rhineland industrial-administrative city, then an inner-London muddle. But look for the housing built at the same time as the new metropolis, and you find that a utopian Southern California was more the model than Düsseldorf or Acton. The Park Hill estate (no relation to its Sheffield namesake) is a particularly remarkable case in point. Planned by Wates, one of the largest commercial volume housebuilders in an era when even they occasionally had pretensions to 'good design', this is one of the leafiest, most luxuriant of suburbs, with either bland little detached houses or vaguely Eric Lyons terraces in amongst mature trees giving way to, extraordinarily, St Bernard's: a secluded 1971 estate of three short terraces by then-famous Swiss high-art architects Atelier 5, in a state of impeccable preservation – the equivalent of Barratt Homes bringing in Peter Zumthor to design part of one of their estates. St Bernard's is built into a hill, with car parks under the houses and pedestrian passageways to the terraces, although signs remind you that the land is, in fact, private, and that you aren't really supposed to be here. The materials are exquisitely used, stock brick and wood treated as luxurious rather than generic. 'Public' gardens are lushly overgrown, meeting the sharp lines of Atelier 5's executive Brutalism. The effect is not particularly European, however; rather it looks as if some of the Case Study Houses designed by Californian Modernists in the 1950s had strayed accidentally into Surrey. Pacific Palisades in Purley.

However, these are exceptional; much more typical is the sprawl around the Borough's centre, those burbs where 'going into town' means going into Croydon, not the West End. Thornton Heath, for instance. Many of these low-rise areas have their terraces, semis and villas suddenly interrupted by office blocks that seem to have got lost on their way from Cannon Street to East Croydon station. One such monster dominates much of Thornton Heath, squat and massively wide. It's also here that the borough's only

notable post-1970s building has just been completed, a library extension by FAT. Their wilful attempts to *épater les architectural bourgeois* mask – or as they would no doubt see it, accentuate – an attention to architecture's social purpose that is unusual in the UK today. Both of these aspects can be seen when you first approach the library. It's the extension to an old Carnegie Library, a pocket-baroque in brick and Portland stone. Their addition is a white box with 'LIBRARY' in supergraphics across the top, the ostensible modernism 'subverted' by an incongruous support, put there as an evocation in concrete of the ubiquitous suburban half-timbering. Drop the 'OMG jokes' reaction for a second (if we're lucky, the architects might eventually do the same), and this is a remarkably serious, not at all whimsical public building, warm, welcoming and on this Tuesday afternoon in May, very well used. Its built-in chairs and sofas look *comfortable*, which is an interestingly rare thing in new architecture. As a building, it's a fantastic snub to the current rash of library closures.

Thornton Heath Library takes a small-scale thing and makes it better, in a place with large-scale problems. Far more common attempts to 'solve' these can be found in the overdeveloped new spec blocks of flats, or Saunders Architects' generic Blairbuild Thornton Heath Leisure Centre, with its swoopy roofs and tinny cladding. Maybe these will survive long enough to acquire central Croydon's unexpected period charm, but making the same mistake twice is somewhat less forgiveable. The London Borough of Croydon has suffered from over a century of non-plan, and the result is chaos – dereliction next to newbuild, dramatically crammed and then almost criminally low-density. It's full of surprises for the walker, but it's a disastrous way to run a city, as the horrendous traffic, or the decidedly tense tenor of public interaction, makes very clear. But what does it say about the South East, suburban England, the area that lords it over the rest of the country? This place is, in theory, a major example of our most powerful, most wealthy, most leafy areas. You'd never guess, though, as it feels like another Britain entirely – a poor but multiracial, intriguing but miserable place which could really do with social planning and social housing, rather than more speculation and a Business Improvement District. Croydon is a *place*. It could be much more of one.

Greater Croydon

The entirely excellent Croydon Tramlink connects the town centre with a large hinterland stretching into the boroughs of Bromley, Merton and Sutton, which can in turn be considered a kind of Greater Croydon. The Tramlink itself is exactly the same sort of entity as the Manchester Metrolink, the Sheffield Supertram or Birmingham's 'Metro' – a tram that partially runs on streets, partially on specially built concrete viaducts, and partially on railway tracks. They called these 'Metrotrams' in the Soviet Union, where they also built opulent futuristic shelters for them. The Tramlink doesn't have these, but it is once again very striking that a London suburb has been in advance of much of the UK's larger cities in the provision of rapid transit. So six months after the first trip out, curious to have a peek at the other Greater Croydon, away from the tense streets of the town centre and Thornton Heath, we took the Tramlink out to Mitcham Junction. On our way we passed the site of the furniture store burnt out in the August riots, with a block of flats-above-shops still charred and boarded up, a reminder of the moment when all that simmering briefly overflowed. The Tram then traverses an unexpected stretch of very heavy industry, a vast site that now seems unevenly divided between warehousing, light industrial units and, mostly, enormous exurban retail units with gapingly wide surface car parks. From here, we set out to see some of the architecture of the future. Or, rather, we went to find two potential forms of voluntaristic urbanism that the future might promise for London and elsewhere.

The London Borough of Sutton, run by Whigs and Tories, is one of the only major local authorities to become an official 'Vanguard Area' of the 'Big Society'. This piece of 'progressive nonsense', as the internal Conservative discussion has it,[11] entails the transfer of formerly remunerated labour over to volunteers, with accompanying swingeing cuts to council budgets and payrolls. Initially seduced by the vaguely co-operative rhetoric, a real city, Liverpool, signed up to be Big Society pioneers; but upon realizing rather belatedly that the Big Society was essentially a not particularly sophisticated cover for throwing public-sector workers out of their jobs and outsourcing services to Serco and Capita, it pulled out, leaving this affluent Outer London Borough (and nearby, even posher Windsor) to do the pioneering by itself. The process, without the cuddly rhetoric, can be seen at its most rapacious in the downsized 'EasyCouncil' in the inner-London borough of Hammersmith and Fulham, where an outright class war is being fought between super-rich incomers and the tenants of its council estates. Sutton has far fewer poor people in it, so is able to stay cuddly, and accordingly it is the Whigs rather than the Tories that dominate the local council. Their approach to the question is best encompassed by the poster you can find on Sutton Council's website, where 'BIG SOCIETY' is in yellow, with a smiley face in the 'O'; 'NOT BIG GOVERNMENT' is in red, with a frowning face in the 'O'. They really do think we're that stupid.

The Future (Optimistic)

In any case the borough is an ambitious one, with various plans for 'sustainable' settlements in Hackbridge and Beddington, and a Big Society focus amongst the waters of Carshalton. Accordingly, there should be a lot to see. Making our way from Mitcham Junction, we proceed to Beddington, home of a complex called BedZED, or in full, Beddington Zero (Fossil) Energy Development. This is an estate of the Peabody Trust, the most famous of the unelected charitable organizations considered more trustworthy custodians of social housing than democratically-controlled local authorities; a 'progressive' side to our contemporary neo-Victorianism. The Trust was founded by a banker, George Peabody, a century and a half ago (which has lately made him the subject for occasional 'when bankers were nice' features and programmes), and is best known for immense, barrack-like cliffs of stock-brick housing across the second half of the nineteenth century, throughout inner London. The demise of council housing left the likes of Peabody as the last line of defence, and its directors, such as Dickon Robinson and latterly Claire Bennie, have been genuine enthusiasts for architecture and planning, which marks them out somewhat. BedZED is perhaps their most all-encompassing twenty-first-century scheme, an early 2000s project whose environmental and social seriousness is admirable, albeit cloaked by an architectural bumptiousness.

It is not exactly blessed with a delightful site. BedZED faces at one corner a large, straggling post-war estate of little wit or imagination, at another a crushingly dull development of '90s mock-Tudor spec flats, and has as its hinterland one of those illusory places where London seems to end entirely, in pylons, brackish marshes and placid horses. It's a long walk from Mitcham Junction Tramlink, or a stroll from Hackbridge station – not exactly remote, but hardly well-connected either. It's a large development by contemporary standards, several rows of flats, accessible from the ground but partly connected by arched metal walkways. Creepers grow over much of it. The design is a superior essay in the now-defunct Blairite idiom (Peabody's most recent estate, finished in early 2012 in Pimlico, reverts to their original yellow-brick monumentality, a sure sign of a shift in architectural culture). There is a lot of wood cladding; there are metal balconies; there is a great deal of glass. There is also some residual 'vernacular', in that the street façades are partly in an industrial red brick. The wood-clad upper storeys have a barrel-shaped overhang, and are topped with solar panels and multicoloured chimneys, a spout-cowl vaguely like a hen's crest. At the edge of the estate is a combined power station running on the estate's own waste, which also has a café and a social centre. The architects, Bill Dunster, and the designers of the energy-generating system, BioRegional, both have offices on site. Most 'sustainable' developments are fudges of various kinds, well-insulated but concrete-framed blocks, but this one really does what it claims; it really is an entire estate that is self-sufficient in energy. Whatever one's opinion of the ethics or political efficacy of 'opting out' of a carbon-generated national grid – my view is probably fairly predictable – this place has had the courage of its convictions. It's notable how it has had practically no successors.

This isn't just the project of some 'green entrepreneurs', though, but in theory a full-scale social housing estate. How much does it actually work as such? It may be foolhardy to make generalizations on brief acquaintance, but there were ample semiotic clues that some might have moved here because of Lifestyle (those growing their own veg on the balconies), and others because they had got lucky on the waiting list (those with St George flags covering most of the floor-to-ceiling windows). Remarkably for a place so surrounded by desolation, there's a lot of people milling around. That might be a consequence of the scheme's density, which feels pretty odd in front of a great big scrubby expanse, but comes over as quite genuinely warm, or maybe that's just by comparison. The most memorable effect is created by the pedestrian route under the arched overhead walkways, where half of what you can see has been overrun by greenery. The car-free spaces feel genuinely permeable and relaxed; you are even trusted to wander around the walkways without any gating. If, as is surely the case, a zero-carbon economy entails a massive new industrial revolution, then this place might be a genuine paragon. Yet it is so obviously an enclave that it's hard to sustain the optimism; it may in fact just be a new incarnation of the cool, exclusive modernist suburbia of St Bernard's, albeit with a 'social' percentage. Libertarian bores might like to complain about sustainability regulations, but the point remains that there is still only one BedZED in the UK, and it's tucked away in Beddington, without a night bus. It's hard to imagine the coalition building more.

The Future (Pessimistic)

As a case in point, neighbouring Hackbridge, which the Whigs are claiming as a 'sustainable suburb', contains two large new blocks in the most banal and debased Urban Renaissance idiom: both taking up tight corner sites, both heavily overdeveloped, both of them just concrete frames encased in 'friendly' yellow-brick cladding. The area around is a particularly odd outer-London landscape, where factories and village closes sit next to each other without the intervention of zoning regulations. As you cross the thin, marshy River Wandle, there is a small, mildly Brutalist estate of low-lying blocks of flats, pebbly concrete and white weatherboarding. Most of them pull back away from the river, leaving a quiet public space where they could have maximized rental value. Then there's an incongruous cul-de-sac of breeze-block flat-roofed cottages in the East Tilbury manner, then an acre or so of achingly Neighbourhood-Watched subtopia, before you eventually arrive in Carshalton.

Carshalton is, I'm told, the real Big Society enthusiast in the area, itching to deregulate and voluntarize itself so long as the TfL buses still pass through. As a village that was evidently swallowed up by London later than many others, this is another place that feels sharply like an enclave, a place carved out by its inhabitants as a way of remaining genteel within the Wen's outer circles. At first it's indistinguishable from the 1930s ribbon development all around, with the PFI college ('Carshalton College – Realising Ambitions') easily imaginable in Hackney. Less typical are the little weatherboarded houses and Garden Suburb closes, and least typical of all is the central feature of Carshalton – its ponds, pretty expanses framed by what looks like one-part fishing village to one-part John Betjeman Surrey utopia. The high street just off here has the sort of picturesque curve and dip that puts an extra few thousand on the price of property; surely those living here put 'Surrey' rather than 'London' on their correspondence, so convincing is the village illusion. Of course some in *this* place enjoy the idea of running their own public services, putting in a bit of time en route to the golf course. A Union Jack hangs from a window in this enclave, to complement the flag of St George in the other enclave at Beddington.

We're now out of Greater Croydon, out of the Tramlink's remit, although ten minutes on the bus takes us to West Croydon's carceral bus station, from which we embark to Valley Park, the site of the former Croydon Power Station, now IKEA. Inner Croydon might feel like a fairly urban and dense place, but that's all absolutely exploded here, just a short distance away. Shed after neon-lit Shed, all of them enormous outlets for sundry retail chains, all of them with a great expanse of car parking in front. It's the exact sort of disurbanism that the last twenty years of planning policy has purported (not always entirely honestly) to oppose, and hence the exact sort that is supposed to pioneer 'recovery', after the planning regulations have been sufficiently dismantled. BedZED and this place are surely diametrically opposed in every possible way, but then it hasn't been unusual over the last two decades to find strip malls abutting sustainable Millennium Villages. Even with that in mind, there's something especially foul about Valley Park, an inescapable pall of menace. The chimneys of the Power Station now decorate IKEA, a place dedicated to *interior* design, to keeping one's own house in order, and letting all outside it go to hell.

Chapter Nine

Plymouth: Fables of the Reconstruction

In Praise of Blitzed Cities

Bombed cities are all different, but they all have a similar feeling. That doesn't mean they're homogeneous, far from it, but that the loss at their heart is similar, if often different in scale. On the far more brutally fought Eastern front, there are several European cities where a tiny proportion of the population can trace their families' presence there further back than the late 1940s. Cities that were wiped out, like Warsaw; cities where an entire population was removed and another population resettled there, like Breslau/Wrocław, Königsberg/Kaliningrad, Lwow/Lviv. In many of the bombed English cities, you feel like this has taken place even when it hasn't – as if the entire city had been vacated and resettled with a whole other group of people having entirely different values and different ways of seeing the world. Sometimes, in the more grandiose of the Blitzed cities, along the walkways of Sheffield or Thamesmead, say, you feel something even harsher – that this new city was built by some race of giants that disappeared, leaving us an environment that's too big, too dramatic, too confident, for the likes of us. Whichever way the question is posed, the bombed cities are still, even now, sixty years later, considered ugly and jarring and 'alien'.

They're incoherent, they're strange, they're dramatic, they're modern, they're messy, they're not 'historic', except for the occasional eerie reconstructed reservation. This is their strength. In the European cities that the Luftwaffe or the RAF didn't do over, you have a nineteenth-century centre ringed by post-war housing, a clear divide between one and the other which curdled over the decades into a strict spatial divide between one sort of people and another sort of people. In the bombed cities, we don't have that – we have council flats next to Regency terraces next to parks conjured up from bomb sites. The super-rich sleep slightly less easily in their beds, erecting gates around their new developments to reflect how unsafe they feel. Tourists shun the new places, described in the guides as 'concrete jungles' and 'monstrous carbuncles'. In the process these once famous forgotten cities have forged some of the strongest, and strangest, identities in the UK.

If you grew up somewhere like this, time feels out of joint. You will have spent your youth watching tall, ultra-modern constructions being knocked down, and brick simulations of Victorian streets that never existed being built in their place. You will have used the loathed public spaces for loitering – hung around in the precincts, drunk cider in the civic amenities, like greasier, pimplier versions of the attenuated watercolour peopleoids that populated the drawings of 1940s planners. The plazas were ringed with charity shops, and it seemed oddly just and fitting – the worn elegance of the post-war city making a dignified withdrawal from the screeching crassness of the giant, exurban American malls. But there is in these cities a double absence. Modernity did continue in a disavowed form, after all, in the almost hidden grandeur of the container port, the gigantic automated spectacle of cranes, tracks and multicoloured boxes that everyone conspires not to look at. Ports were supposedly about the nautical tourism that filled the derelict docks, the reminiscence over the days when sailors actually got off the boat, not this awesome robotic spectacle with its practically invisible workers. A third loss is only just slowly starting to be registered – the loss of the socialist spirit that impelled us to redesign our chaotic, profiteering cities as something unified, public and civic, without gates, fences or hierarchies. The centre of Plymouth is one of the UK's most spectacular places to feel this. At the heart of it is one great ensemble.

England's Last Great Street

When you arrive, it's blocked off by a car park, and shadowed by a clearly once shiny but now greying glass office block; but you find it soon enough. It starts with a series of underpasses. These aren't your common or garden subways, but wide, open things, a sort of combination of underpass and grand public square. Pass under them and you're right in the middle of an axis, flanked by large, severe Portland stone buildings. The space is vast, something which subsequent planners have tried to efface by dint of everything from funfairs to gardens to giant TV screens. Stylistically, this boulevard is not quite classical, but not quite modernist either; for that, you must walk all the way to the end, where you'll find three towers. On the axis is a Guildhall, Romanesque mixed with Mid-Century Modern, and a high-rise Civic Centre, elegant, well-made and almost derelict. Further on is a bland and shoddy Holiday Inn, very much occupied, but that passes unnoticed, because you're then at the Hoe, a wide public park looking out over a glorious waterfront. The panoramic view takes in warships, rolling green hills and rocky Cornish cliffs, and you have a lighthouse, a lido, and an art deco war memorial for company. The whole thing is one continuous, planned piece of urbanism. This is Armada Way, the main street of Plymouth city centre.

It's the axial fulcrum of a comprehensive plan, in the British city more damaged than any other by Luftwaffe attacks. Patrick Abercrombie's masterplan was not especially avant-garde – certainly a lot less so than his plans for London – and nor was the architecture. It's in a style which is as yet un-named, some sort of Attlee-Scando-Stalino-classicism, which anyone familiar with a Broadmead, a Moor or an Above Bar will recognize; though it is superior to all of these, avoiding their fudges and compromises. Architecturally, it lacks the futurity of near-contemporaries such as London's ultra-modernist Churchill Gardens or popu-list Lansbury Estate, or the multilevel replanning of Coventry. Its compatriots are elsewhere – Auguste Perret's Le Havre, or, rather more controversially, post-war East Berlin or Warsaw. A big boulevard for the tanks to go down (this is a garrison town after all), symmetrical stone buildings, ceremonial plazas. It's not what 1950s critics considered 'the architecture of democracy'. At this distance, however, its insistence on the traditional street seems more contemporary, as does its Continental nature – a space seemingly designed for cafés to spill out onto the pavement, which, in good weather – we're here in June – they do. If, for Aldo Rossi, Berlin's Stalinallee was 'Europe's last great street', then Armada Way is certainly Britain's last.

It's also a counterfactual in stone. Abercrombie's Plymouth is what might have happened everywhere in the UK if serious, ideological modernism had never enjoyed its brief moment of planning hegemony, with its concrete and glass and its new approach to planning. Plymouth's driving ideas are those of inter-war, twilight-of-empire Britain, as are its architects – Thomas Tait, William Crabtree, Louis de Soissons, Giles Gilbert Scott. The influences of Edwin Lutyens's New Delhi, or Charles Holden's Orwellian Senate House in Bloomsbury are also palpable. It's curious that the architectural historian and campaigner Gavin Stamp, for instance, has recently repeated the claim that 1940s–50s Plymouth brought little of value to replace the destroyed city, given that it represents exactly what he has been arguing for in British architecture and planning for some decades. These dignified masonry buildings, in a non-dogmatic classical tradition, are equally far from Le Corbusier and Leon Krier. But strangely enough, central Plymouth is seemingly held in no greater public affection than the more hard-line Coventry or Sheffield. Invariably, the plan is described as a 'concrete jungle' in circles non-architectural, despite the fact that the dominant materials are Portland stone, granite and brick. It's a reminder that modernity and planning itself, not its stylistic vagaries, are what offend a certain kind of British psyche. It is not *pretty*. In spirit it may be nearer to Georgian Bath than anything else designed in the twentieth century, but central Plymouth is not picturesque, and some will never forgive it for that.

What it does prove, however, is that this modernized classicism was tired by the late 1940s. Some individual buildings are very impressive – the two stepped department stores which provide the axis's main focus, by Tait and Alec French, are loomingly

powerful as anything from the 1930s, and B. C. Sherren's National
Provincial Bank is lovely, and its stripped classical columns and
Scandinavian blue-tiled clock tower are remarkably similar to the
precisely contemporary Finland Station in Leningrad. Overall,
though, it is the cohesiveness, planting and sheer generosity of
space that are really of value here. The architecture represents an
aesthetic in its dotage. In a very prominent place is Giles Gilbert
Scott's last completed church, a sadly thin, wan, provincial design
from the architect of such monstrous masterpieces as Battersea
Power Station and Liverpool's Anglican Cathedral.

In some ways, central Plymouth is a reminder of just how
necessary modernism was. The turn to modernism within the
Abercrombie Plan, in slightly later structures like the Civic
Centre and the wonderful Pannier Market, reflect this feeling
of relative lightness and ease, especially in the whale-like concrete interior of the latter. After the 1960s, the grand civic gesture
sometimes continued in a different form; Peter Moro's late 1970s
Theatre Royal is central Plymouth's only real Brutalist building, and an excellent one, its geometrical complexity and harsh
volumes akin more to Moro's ex-Tecton partner Lasdun than to
his own more clipped work. Nearby, The Pavilions is a messily

ambitious structure where pedways link a swimming pool to a car park, shopping and then back to the Abercrombie centre, a laudably sweeping undertaking marred by cheap and nasty '80s retail detailing. After this, not much, but it's a formidable ensemble, of worldwide significance. Like nineteenth-century Glasgow, or twentieth-century Sheffield or Coventry, Plymouth doesn't seem to know how important it is as a piece of urbanism and a place for architecture. In fact, it seems bent on trying to destroy the things that make it important. The Civic Centre was very nearly demolished, listed (against the council's own opposition) before it could be levelled for a shopping mall. The edges of the Abercrombie Plan are frayed, a mix of dereliction and dross.

Stare Miasto

Plymouth is lucky enough to have both one of the UK's most complete pieces of grand city planning and one of the most interesting, albeit slightly sanitized, areas of ad hoc inner-urban townscape. Walk round the breathtaking panorama of the Hoe past the high walls of an inadvertently proto-Brutalist fortress, still used by the military, and you're in the Barbican, an area once slated for demolition, but restored by the Civic Trust movements of the 1960s and 70s. It's full of passages and alleys, strange and surprising vernacular architecture and, interestingly, very sensitive modernist infill. Plymouth evidently had one of the best post-war City Architects in Hector Stirling, and his Paton Watson Quadrate is a lovely council estate of lush, bright stone, tile-hanging, Swedish details and easy informality, a remarkable contrast with the Baron Haussmann melodrama of Armada Way or Royal Parade just a few yards away. Along the alleys of tea shops and ice-cream parlours you can find almost cubistic mini-blocks of flats next to the half-timbering. Sadly, all this cleverness and warmth gives way further along Sutton Harbour to the luxury architecture of the 1990s and 2000s, with several more-or-less miserable blocks of flats, crowded onto their sites. Sometime in the 1970s or 1980s Plymouth seemed to lose all its confidence, seemed to start to hate itself. It's a familiar enough story in the north of England, and deindustrialized, poor, shabby but often glorious old Plymouth

has more in common with a Bradford or a Liverpool than with the seaside, spa and silicon towns of the South.

The place's reputation, its Pilgrim Fathers-related fame, doesn't translate much into self-esteem, let alone tourism. The Barbican has its art galleries and boutiques, but I'm told that they change hands at a rapid rate. There's no naval or maritime museum, no self-commemoration, and perhaps the still-existing functions of the place are the reason for this. The Royal Navy still have their base in Devonport, off-limits to the public; ships are still built in Plymouth, albeit without a particularly large work-force, and this may keep the city from dying entirely, but it also helps to keep it lumpen. You see it in the Union Jack T-shirts you can buy in Pannier Market, with 'OUR PLACE – OUR BASE' on them. You can see it in the posters for boxing at the Guildhall, where ten pasty pugilists pose as if about to smack you in the mouth. You could find local pride in it, of course, but it still faces the central problem of the working-class city that votes Tory: that it is loyal to its natural enemies, that it sides with its oppressor. Nonetheless, the gradual closure of some parts of the dockyard opens up another potential Plymouth, one that briefly shared in the abortive Urban Renaissance.

Stonehouse boasts a development by Mancunian hipster entrepreneurs Urban Splash, a giant loft conversion of John Rennie's
severe classical King William Victualling Yard. It is, by the standards of this developer, atypically sensitive. Unlike the modernist
buildings they have redeveloped, it has survived without ano-
dized aluminium cladding, without any lime green or hot pink,
which is a tribute of sorts to Plymouth's conservationists. I had
the honour of staying in one of these buildings with friends, two
Polish architects who proceeded to list the problems they had
with the detailing. If you didn't mind the tiny size of the place
and the fact that the windows and floors seemed to be deliberately designed to minimize light, it was very pleasant. The Urban
Splash flags all round the development adjoin the usual middle-
class cafés and bars, although somewhat sparse on the ground.
When you reach the gate that leads out of the Victualling Yard,
the appeal of the place becomes obvious – its previous function
means that it's a community coming pre-gated. It looks out onto
an earlier version of luxury waterside living, the last of the modernist buildings in Plymouth – an apartment block, Ocean Court,
a zippy '70s sci-fi irregular ziggurat. It's the sort of thing you
might find in Benidorm. Adjacent are a couple of surviving sheds
that put together warships and yachts. Normally, this would be an
area of great tension, but the middle-class enclaves in Plymouth
are so small that class cleansing seems a long way off, at least
until prejudice lifts and the south-western bourgeoisie realize
how lovely a city they have in their midst.

One reason for this prejudice, other than ignorance, can surely
be found in the way that the planned Plymouth connects with
the residential areas around it. The joins are drastically unpretty.
Stonehouse itself, while never quite as regular as some of its south-
western near-neighbours, is an area of elegant classical terraces,
with outbreaks of pillared formality in amongst houses painted
in multiple bright colours, as in Bristol. Some have a Georgian
rectitude, some evoke a fishing village more than a big city, but
the effect is relaxed and, like the Abercrombie Plan, European.
The bombsite infill produced by the city council under Hector
Stirling is completely Swedish. Four-storey blocks on a Y-shaped
plan, pitched roofs, simple details, large balconies and communal

gardens enclosed by rubble-stone walls. They don't continue the lines of terraces, but feel of a piece with them nonetheless. Then you meet the mess that divides Stonehouse from the city centre. A large branch of Aldi, of the expected architectural repugnance, reveals itself to be boarded up. A high street leads to the centre, but it's in a wretched state of disrepair. The Grand Theatre pub, an art nouveau gin palace, has a tree growing out of it – as does the building next door, a former Furniture Warehouse. The Grand Theatre itself is a fantastical music hall unlike everything else in Plymouth, and features on its façade panels depicting scenes of imperial and naval triumph. It too appears to be falling apart – the whole street just seems to have been forgotten, the natural link between the residential areas and the centre abandoned to a degree where it almost feels post-apocalyptic. Then a sorry roundabout, like the planned centre on an Aldi budget, leads eventually to the Market and the main streets. The ubiquitous dual carriageways efface any attempt at coherence. The Barbican, Stonehouse and the Centre are all great pieces of urbanism, but linking them together would mean curbing the car – something which Plymouth City Council, mindful of income from its car parks, has no intention of doing.

Plymouth Rock Would Land on Them

The little redevelopment there is in the centre tends to be neither as elegant as in Stonehouse nor as identikit as around Sutton Harbour. Instead there are two structures which have a good pop at the 'iconic'. One is Chapman Taylor's notorious Drake Circus mall, a one-time winner of Building Design's Carbuncle Cup award. It covers and swallows an entire chunk of Abercrombie's Portland stone street, and takes a hard line on photographers. What is most embarrassing is the way it meets one of those straggling landscapes just outside of the centre. The bombed-out Charles Church, left under the Abercrombie Plan as a war memorial on a roundabout, must already have felt strange and marooned. It is surely even more so now that it is framed with giant yellow Trespa wafers. This part is of course the iconic bit, the past-and-present-meeting-in-harmony moment, where the blown-up face of a Primark model looms over the spire, just so we know who is in charge. Its other façade is an obnoxious, windowless car park which faces a 'public' square; facing that is Henning Larsen's Roland Levinsky Building for the University, containing classrooms, offices and studios. Like many an industrial town, Plymouth has a large and expanding ex-Poly, or rather an ex-Poly that was expanding before the introduction of £9,000 tuition fees. The town evidently has a fair degree of hostility to the gown, and even more so – remember this is OUR PLACE, OUR BASE – to the foreign students that pay the largest fees. Perhaps the only time Plymouth has made national news in recent years is when shops here began displaying signs: 'ONLY ONE FOREIGN STUDENT AT A TIME'.

Perhaps mindful of its controversial status in a naval town, the University decided to make a Big Statement here, to which end they hired the well-respected Danish firm Henning Larsen, presumably recognizing the Scandinavian provenance of much post-1945 Plymouth. Or maybe they just hoped for a nice big iconic building. With its combination of gestural vernacular and angular regen shape-making, it's of its time, to say the least, although it genuinely attempts to make something of its prominent site, a decent attempt at civic presence. After I wrote not entirely critically of this building, several employees of the University took issue. One corrected me as follows: 'It was a sketch design from two young architects in the Henning Larsen office with no experience of planning at that scale and no completed buildings under their belts. It was then "value engineered" by BDP Bristol who were novated to the main contractor, HBG … full of good intentions but woefully unresolved to the point that it is near impossible to use for its intended functions and, worse, impossible to adapt to new functions. The shape making does successfully fulfil (the building's) one intention – that of making a space to instantly impress would-be new students and (importantly) their parents or guardians. Beyond that, it fails at many levels – not the least of which is its environmental performance which, since the sketch design put all-glass façades on the south and north elevations, cannot be improved. When it was finished it was already twenty years out of date.'

Drake Circus and the Levinsky building, though neither with great success, do at least try and make something specific to Plymouth. This is in fact enshrined in the city's planning policy – they commissioned a plan from David Mackay, who had planned Barcelona in the 1990s, an astute choice given the sweeping boulevard they would be dealing with. Mackay praised the Abercrombie Plan as 'a masterpiece', proposing only incremental changes to the road system and the rigid zoning of the original plan. Accordingly, Drake Circus's wholesale mallification aside, there are only little encroachments into the planned centre, but all of an extremely low quality – prefab hotels, already dated Blairite apartment blocks, a particularly miserable little casino on the site of a cinema. The council themselves evidently have little affection for the original plan, nor seemingly for Mackay's updating of it, to judge by the refusal to tame the traffic, or their attempt to demolish their own headquarters, the Civic Centre. More encouragingly, the zoning that makes the place so dead on nightfall is being lifted – one of Tait's great towers is now student flats, inadvertently giving ubiquitous developers Unite their only architecturally notable building. The changes to public space are stranger. While there's some effective repavings, that make an otherwise shabby city feel incongruously clean in places, it all leads to the gigantic video screen in the middle of the axis to Armada Way, as if to remind shoppers that they aren't that far from the TV. There's always something a little dystopian about a huge TV screen in a public space, and this one is no exception.

Planned post-war Plymouth is now being recognized as having value, with revisionist publications, such as Jeremy Gould's excellent *Plymouth: Vision of a Modern City*, a map and website, *20th Century City*, several listings by English Heritage, and the possibility of the centre being made a conservation area. It's about time that social democratic Britain was the subject of something more than giggling and ridicule, and there's no doubt that the incremental demolitions of decent buildings around the edges of the place and their replacement with dross should be stopped. Yet that the centre should become an object for Keep Calm and Carry On austerity tourism, or that the dockyards might all get Urban Splashed, both seem equally unlikely. It remains a naval base, gradually and attritionally being replaced by a shopping base for affluent towns in Devon and Cornwall. Plymouth already has its post-industrial leisure, its riverside galleries and loft conversions, and yet remains poor; and the results in other cities that have favoured this approach are hardly encouraging. It needs new ideas, that aren't tied up entirely with bringing in middle-class residents or shoppers. But as a place to come and think about alternatives, you could do a lot worse than this forlorn, bracing city.

Chapter Ten

Oxford: Quadrangle and *Banlieue*

So You Went to the Other Place?

The Thames Gateway, as noted in Chapter 1, is an attempt to divert the growth of London eastwards. There's one major reason for this, aside from the dozens of deindustrialized sites along the Thames's eastern reaches – the fact that London has spent the last few decades expanding rapidly to the west, entirely under its own steam. To the rail passenger, it has expanded along the old Great West Railway which travellers will now know as First Great Western, who provide in-train entertainment panels, as if you're on a transatlantic flight rather than a train to Bracknell. To the driver, it has expanded along the line of the M4 motorway, a 'corridor' that stretches as far as Swansea; and to the wherryman, the Wen's pustules are creeping directly up the River Thames. Given that here, the New Britain cleaves sharply to the train line, a trip on FGW is one of the few times that the non-driver can really get a view of the place in its purest form. The westward train passes first along the route to Heathrow, then past the industrial and suburban town of Slough, with its outgrowth of Blairite tower blocks by the station. It passes through the compellingly horrible vistas of Reading, where you have a front-line seat for one of the more comprehensively remade recent cities: train-side business parks with delicate, expensive architecture that looks authentically Californian; sad, shoddy Blair-era yuppiedromes; 'iconic' office skyscrapers that look suspiciously empty, and then the grim, blasted remains of a Victorian factory town. The green belt is next interrupted by the inexplicable montage of cooling towers and Barratt Noddyhomes in Didcot, and after that by the giant edge-city factories of Swindon. If the 'new economy' – at least in terms of software, research, high-tech – really exists as anything other than the organized fraud of property speculation and 'financial services', then it exists here. That the Thames Valley is the locus for this makes clear that the geographical spread of power in the new economy is exactly the same as it was in the old – a route which runs, essentially, between London and Oxford.

Oxford is not ostensibly high-tech in the same way as Cambridge, whose 'Silicon Fen' is signposted by the science parks on its outskirts. Oxford remains a Harry Potter playground in its heart, although it somehow coexists as a dying Midlands industrial town, another important difference with its East Anglian competitor. The Oxford–London corridor of power dominates British politics as much as it ever has. If it isn't the ignorant, coked-up thugs of the Bullingdon Club on the government benches, it's the earnest ex-PPE students and Oxford Union debaters on the opposition bench. Oxford is, not to put too fine a point on it, enemy territory. It also has some staggeringly beautiful architecture, of various centuries, so it would seem necessary to take its temperature – and to compare official 'Oxford' with the Oxford of the car factories and the Oxford of Blackbird Leys, an 'overspill' estate which is one of the poorest in the UK. Oxford is rare in containing within it both of the two factions of British capitalism, both landed old money and industrial new money, although the absence of industry and the smug dominance of the University would suggest that there is really no contest.

I arrived in Oxford armed with Nikolaus Pevsner's unfinished, recently reassembled opus *Visual Planning and the Picturesque*, a work where the great Hegelian topographer wanders round Oxford, Lincoln's Inn in London and Roehampton's Alton Estate, seeing all of them as exemplars of an irregular, organic approach to planning based on juxtaposition and flow rather than orders and axes, that he sees – debatably, but interestingly – as a quintessentially English approach to towns. It's a valid way of planning a city, no doubt, but Oxford as a whole has certain large-scale differences with how most of the cities I like work.

An early, easy but exemplary moment is the approach from the railway station. Like Cambridge, Oxford is based on making sure industrial modernity doesn't intrude too far into the heart of the city, so that your first sight of one of the world's most famous cities is a station like a 1980s shopping centre, a car park, and some volume housebuilders' dreck. The cities that look exciting from the train – in this book, Birmingham, Brighton, Edinburgh, Newport – pitch you straight into the city and its bridges, office blocks and spires. There have been minor attempts to rectify this in Oxford in recent years, specifically in the Saïd Business School. Irrespective of its function, the design by Dixon Jones is fascinating, in the faintly chilling and painterly Mediterranean style common to Aldo Rossi and Giorgio de Chirico, a brick colonnade with a stepped, stylized copper tower. It's a start.

You've Got to Hide Your Modernism Away

Oxford's most 'picturesque' moments are also spectacularly exclusive: the majority of the spaces catalogued in Pevsner's study are basically private quadrangles, open only at the colleges' discretion. I'm here with a student who has a swipe card, a tellingly security-conscious concession to modernity which gets us into practically everywhere, enabling him to give me one of the most rewarding tours of modern architecture available in the UK – yet through a form of urbanism that seems alien to the open city post-war modernism promised. The college, courtyard and quadrangle system has direct consequences for the modern architecture of Oxford. While in Cambridge there are places such as the Sidgwick Site, where modernism takes centre stage, there's nothing of the sort in its Thames-side competitor, although there is a great deal to discover. It's all post-war, it's all very good, and it's nearly all hidden away where the tourists won't look. So, at St John's College you might enter through an authentically medieval courtyard, after a little while you will come to something like the Beehives. These were the first Modernist buildings in town, designed in the '50s by the Architects Co-Partnership at a time when most of Oxford's new buildings were neo-Georgian. They're accommodation for students, detailed in a clipped, hard stone, with miniature spires at the peaks. But the ethos was different, not solely in its modernity – the architects were a co-operative, sincerely committed to the new social democratic Britain, and the effect is not at all hierarchical.

What does this matter, though, when it is inserted into such a hierarchical system?

The Harold Wilson Labour governments' intent seemed to be making a more meritocratic ruling class by opening up education to gifted working-class youth, encouraging a real social mobility which did, it should be admitted, differ from the property-based inducements of Thatcher and Blair. While this tended to occlude the possibility of getting rid of the class system altogether, it at least offered to create a more permeable and dynamic version of class society. Modernism, when it belatedly arrived in Oxford, followed the rules of an inherently exclusive and undemocratic city, vaguely attempting to infuse it with a more democratic sense of space and style. As they're fundamentally unchallenged by it, the colleges treat it very well. For all the high-profile crowing about controversial structures such as James Stirling's Florey Building, here you will find no spalling concrete, no rusting steel windows, no falling red tiles. Curiously, the process of incrementally adding spatially 'new' annexes to the quadrangles continued after modernism, in an even more self-conscious fashion.

In St John's College, prickly Brutalist quadrangles by Arup give way to early-90s postmodernism by MacCormac Jamieson Pritchard. As if to reinforce the Lewis Carroll feel, there's a giant chessboard in their stock-brick assemblage of amphitheatres and walkways. These structures continue modernism's insights into space – there's movement here above and below, multiple levels, passageways and trapdoors, all of which would never be allowed somewhere that was to be Secured by Design. It's welcoming, surprising and flowing space, if you're allowed in. But all this is emphatically not public. My friend's electronic touch-card is here applied to a tiny, spiked door. In fact, in subscribing to its essentials while subverting its stylistic unity, modernism and Pomo might just have been following in the footsteps of the various deliberately crass and aggressive Ruskinians of the nineteenth century – like William Butterfield's buildings at Keble College, an industrial red-brick fireworks display beamed down from Cottonopolis or Brum, which is perhaps more of an attack on Oxonian assumptions than anything in concrete. This in turn leads to one of the most extraordinary examples of the city's stealth modernism,

Ahrends Burton and Koralek's snaking high-tech extension, a remarkable brown-glass tentacle thrown out along a lawn, a bit of which was later snipped off by the prolifically boring Rick Mather Architects, purveyors of sickeningly tasteful modernist refurbishments to the Ashmolean Museum and elsewhere.

When you finally emerge from the secrecy and privacy, the architectural enclosure and excitement of the quadrangular system, Oxford becomes less dense, less full of surprises, and feels more like Cambridge: straggling, suburban, dotted with landmarks. One of these is a gigantic Brutalist laboratory by the modern architect most associated with Cambridge, Leslie Martin. Weirdly, where everyone can see it, it's in a far more parlous state than every other bit of Oxford Modern – as if the owners want to punish it for presumptuousness in being both modern and actually visible to the civilian. The concrete is worn, and a tragically cheap PFI extension in blue Trespa has been added at the corners and on top. Next to this is a Leslie Martin building in far better nick, the Libraries. This is in the first book about architecture I ever bought, a 1960s Pelican *History of English Architecture*, where they describe it as 'dynastic' – which sounds about right. Somewhere between Hilversum and Assyria, though my guide suggests Odessa. From there, along gaping voids of playing fields, we come to St Catherine's College, Arne Jacobsen's Grade 1 listed High Modernist opus.

The entrance to it is by Stephen Hodder, which sits uneasily between Jacobsen's obsessively composed elegance and a more timid, business-park-like pseudomodernism. Pevsner would surely have regarded this attempt to fit in as a big mistake, a misreading of the picturesque qualities of Oxford planning. St Catherine's, being designed by an internationally famous Dane and all, is often considered offensively un-English. Which is funny, as the first thing it makes me think of, in its ruthless rectilinear sweep set amongst greenery, is the Hunstanton School by Alison and Peter Smithson: a tough, sleek, American-influenced design, which as a Secondary Modern catered for a rather different post-war educational clientele. Both have something very Alexander Pope about them – measured, unnatural, Augustan. I prefer not to use the term High Modernism, considering it pernicious and often meaningless, but if it means anything in architecture it means this, as sure as it means Woolf or Eliot in literature. It proclaims itself as a Work of Art, and emphatically *not* a popular one, whereas modernism on the whole is usually engaged, whatever some may try to prove, in a constant, if tortured, dialogue with the popular. Being 'High', St Catherine's eschews montage and juxtaposition, standing on its own. Yet if it does have anything to do with Oxford it's in the *Alice* element, the miniature mazes of topiary that define and demarcate the space.

As a focus, a monument, an attempt to set up a new version of a dreaming spire, St Catherine's has a concrete tower. This too evokes something Italian and eerily Rationalist. While the Saïd Business School suggests de Chirico, this closely resembles the Sant'Elia Memorial in Como, northern Italy, designed under Mussolini by the fascist modernist Guiseppe Terragni, although it's significantly more trim and chic than anything the Italian Futurists cooked up. There is nothing particularly English in this, nothing picturesque, although it perhaps suggests that the architectural influence of the Grand Tour endured into the mid-twentieth century. St Catherine's is a fascinating series of well-made monuments, and I could look at this place for hours, but – and here I conform appallingly to English stereotype – I could never love it. Pevsner did, which is strange, as although it accords with his liking for a low-voltage, rationalized modernism, it's not remotely connected to the 'placeness' of Oxford, except perhaps in its expense. Out from here, we hit some postmodernism of a much more typical kind than the thoughtful spatial manipulations of a Richard MacCormac – a villa with a Victorian roofline, Georgian coursing and Thatcherite brickwork.

Class and the Picturesque in Oxford City Centre

The centre, in as much as it's possible to speak of a centre in Oxford, arranges itself around magnificent baroque constructions by Wren, Gibbs, Hawksmoor. No revisionism here – they are wonders of architecture, and wonders in the relationship of buildings to each other – but nobody needs reminding of this fact. We're here while the students are on holiday, and there are many people other than me snapping away avidly at the Radcliffe Camera and All Souls. It's so funny how Modern architects, when they were commissioned to build here, conformed to this place and didn't want to disrupt it. The tiny Holywells shop was designed by Glasgow Brutalists Andy MacMillan and Isi Metzstein, architects capable of great aggression and wilfulness – but here, they slotted into the streetline a building so delicate, small-scale and unassuming that even Charles Windsor couldn't possibly object. I imagine that a hypothetical Prince-sympathizing reader of *Visual Planning and the Picturesque* would find it difficult to discern the picturesque, the visual drama and humanism, in Pevsner's later examples such as the Alton council estate in South West London, simply because of its function – because it's a series of mere council blocks and maisonettes, no matter how intelligently, windingly or haphazardly organized. If I were being consistent, I would refuse to respond in kind to these little side streets, as where a series of contrasting rooflines along a narrow pathway lead to a bristling Hawksmoor spire – but the cultural signifiers rub me up the wrong way, grate at my inverted snobbery: the olde worlde typeface, the taint of Hogwarts, the cutesy advert selling a '17th Century Hotel'. Such whimsy can in places be invigorating and annoying in irksome measure, as with the neo-Venetian 'Bridge of Sighs' that spans one street, dated 1914. The fantasy is here, at least, entirely convincing. Pevsner proclaims of this site that 'a bridge across a street is always the greatest temptation to explore beyond'. We thought better of it.

It's interesting to see how the three biggest egos in 1960s British architecture – James Stirling and Alison and Peter Smithson – inserted their ideas into all this. We don't see the interior courtyard of Stirling's Florey Building for Queen's College. We couldn't, though a helpful sign read 'ARCHITECTS WHO WANT TO SEE THE OUTSIDE OF THIS BUILDING MUST HAVE PRIOR PERMISSION FROM THE HOME BURSAR'. Extraordinary, really – the assumption is that only architects would want to see one of the most famous buildings by the most famous twentieth-century British architect, one so well-known that even the televised Stirling Prize is named after him; imagine at the Asmolean, 'artists who want to see this painting must have prior permission'. Here, Oxford merely makes explicit, with its customary bullish, privilege-ridden confidence, what the rest of the country so often assumes. Only architects like architecture (because what you're looking at in the Radcliffe Camera isn't architecture, it's *Heritage*). Via nosing round and trespassing we see enough to, once again, observe how much more massive Stirling's buildings look in photographs than in reality, and to note what a poor bit of planning it is – surrounded by a car park and straggly indeterminate space, taking the Oxonian fixation with hiding away to outrageous extremes. This is, equally tellingly, not Stirling's fault – his plans specified a river walk alongside the building, but the College were not enthused by such dangerous public-spiritedness. The internal space looks wonderful through the grate, though the floor-to-ceiling windows may still be a more empirical reason for unpopularity.

All that said, it's an extremely impressive building. As a piece of stand-alone architecture it has more in common with Butterfield at Keble than anything else, full of colour, tensions and angles. It's a shame that it got plonked in this corner, when it could have been placed somewhere where its postures could have been *aimed* at something, rather than a private matter. Maybe it does do this from above. It loses Picturesqueness points for good reason, not so much visually – Pevsner clearly couldn't stand the more militant modernisms such as Brutalism, expressionism and constructivism, all of which are drawn on by Stirling here – but for its lack of interest in the spirit of the place. It's curious then to note that the Smithsons – who were, in the architectural press of the 1950s, the scourge of Townscape and picturesque planning – did something so mild and contextual. Their halls for St Hilda's are stone-clad, composed and serene. Like many of their buildings (even Robin Hood Gardens, in a way), there's an uneasy attempt to do two seemingly contradictory things. The buildings themselves are austere and not at all ingratiating, deliberately inorganic. Across this they stretch a wooden trellis to encourage planting, to encourage something ad hoc and accidental. It's a fairly arid exercise in dialectic, resulting in no real tension or spark, but the relative softness of the approach compared to their social housing says curious things about the architects' sense of priorities. Social housing was to be raw and powerful, Oxford colleges tame and retiring. There's nothing necessarily wrong with this – which should inspire more pride? – but the residents of Robin Hood Gardens were given no trellises to invite greenery across the streets in the sky. Not, to be fair, that the council would have maintained any planting.

Non-collegiate residential planning in Oxford is another contrast with Cambridge, again showing something denser and more cohesive. Near the Ashmolean, or especially in the planned enclave of Park Town, you can find some exceptionally orderly classical planning. Not having been to Bath, I don't expect terraces in the south of England to look this ordered and elegant, and grope around for northern comparisons to make sense of them. Halifax, perhaps, which is around the same size. Near to the stone terraces you will find occasional modernist incursions into the actual streetline, only a couple of which the tourists can see. Spindly, Gothic Brutalism from Arup can suddenly interrupt the space of ruling-class comfort, but it recovers instantly from the blow. Oxford keeps its modernity closely guarded, as secretive and exclusive as you'd expect for a place which is still a dominant locus of power – in media, in politics, in the City, wherever – in the UK, even after nearly 900 years. Beautiful as it may be, it's a pity nobody has ever really tried to threaten it: whether for modernist architects or socialist politicians, the aim was reform rather than revolution. We suffer for that lack of mettle.

Oxford in the West Midlands

As befits a city closer to Coventry than to London, Oxford's other half is of the West Midlands, not of the South East. A friend who grew up in Oxford, spoiled by the presence of the dreaming spires, remembered as his first experience of real excitement at architecture a glass bridge at the Morris Cowley works, where you could watch the cars being transported from one end of the factory to the other, above you. This has long since been demolished, but if you're interested in finding that other Oxford, it's in an almost straight line east from the centre. You can get a taste of it from the Westgate Centre, which is along with the not particularly admirable Oxfordshire County Council offices the most prominent modern structure in central Oxford. The shopping mall itself is of little note, its double-height spaces jazzed up with neo-Georgian details, but the back-end service area shows a radically different conception of the picturesque. I'm not altogether joking: someone really thought out these spaces, really planned their arrangement and spatial organization.

The best way to see this is going round the arse end of the city centre, past one of the twenty-first century's few architectural contributions to Oxford, a Wetherspoons as pseudomodern palazzo. Then you find the car park, whose buckling concrete floors are each given pitched-roofed corners, stacked on top of each other, which may well be a gesture at contextualism. A skybridge goes from the car park to the shopping mall, which may or may not have been better if a copy of the Venetian Bridge of Sighs. The main interest is in the circulation spaces at the corner, where there is pedestrian access to the walkway. Long-disused yellow escalators, '60s signage, vividly shaped concrete forms painted white and seldom repainted, the faint smell of urine – classic British modernism. The floors flow into each other, and at every level you get a sense of the entire complex all at once, with thin, elegant concrete supports running between pedestrian ramps. There is picturesque planning inside, but maybe not in the way the building connects with the area around, which is somewhat lacking in tact.

The route – and it is an easy route, you can do the whole thing on the number 5 bus – goes almost entirely down the exact same road. That road is, first, High Street, or in Oxon parlance 'The High', the part of picturesque collegiate Oxford that is most accessible to the townie. It's a series of screens, perimeter walls with Gothic or baroque detail, containing the gateways to various colleges; the vertical punctuation as the street curves around, the spires and towers, are usually within those walls, not outside of them. It is not formal, however; retail buildings, often with cantilevered bay windows, are interspersed. Then you come to a roundabout, again in typically annoying Oxon parlance known as The Plain, and Cowley Road. Eventually, this road gets you to Blackbird Leys. But before it does, you watch

Oxford evaporating with great speed, being replaced first with a shabby-genteel Trustafarian enclave, then with 1930s suburbia of the most identikit kind. Cowley Road is long and not entirely straight, but the accidents of the free market have not managed to create something as interesting as the accidents of feudalism. It is a category error to lambast an arterial road for not resembling a central high street, but the difference is nonetheless sharp.

There's little worth noting on the Cowley Road, but for two colourful moments. A one-storey parade of takeaways has been decorated with lurid 'graf', of the day-glo sort you might get in Bristol – ergo, vibrancy. Opposite is East Oxford NHS Centre, designed by Hunter and Partners for PFI vultures Carillion. To get some idea of how low public and governmental esteem for architecture might be, the high status of the NHS (such that even attacks on it like Andrew Lansley's part-privatization bill have to be phrased as continuations or fulfilments rather than repudiations of it) has never really translated into decent NHS architecture. The mega-hospitals of the '60s were never, with a couple of exceptions, great works of design; their eventual successors in the 2000s even less so, due to the strictures of PFI. That's of course fine, if form follows function, but in East Oxford

Health Centre the design is clumsily gesturing for attention. If the bright blue render, Alsopian pilotis and bolted-on wood are standard New Labour-era components, the continuous wave of the roof set against the length and rectilinearity of the rest of the building is especially unfortunate. It was apparently completed in 2007, but there's a concrete mixer and a fenced-off area in the forecourt. Then there's a huge '30s cinema (now, like so many of them, an Evangelical church), and nothing thereafter of interest until you get to Templars Square.

Class and the Picturesque in Blackbird Leys

Cowley, if seen as an independent town (which it isn't, not even legally) has at its centre a place which is not awful, not disastrous, neither hideously ugly nor hideously dilapidated, but nonetheless particularly depressing. Templars Square houses the pound shops you don't get in Oxford proper, a bookie's, a New Look and a Co-op. In design terms, it has a vertical feature detailed in white tile, while the rest of it plumps for a brick-infill mild modernism. This being Oxford, it's often evoked with a shudder as some sort of monstrous carbuncle, but it's a lot less interesting than that. Low-rise council and private houses start to be supplanted by flats, Y-plan 1950s council flats, and then a bridge passes a freight railway, forming a very precise boundary. You could put a railway station here for Blackbird Leys, but curiously nobody has thought to do so. From the top deck of the aforementioned number 5 bus, you can see the panorama of the estate, low-rise but for two tall towers, and just beyond it, the remains of the Cowley car factories, most of which has been redeveloped as business parks, retail parks and such, leaving a relatively small BMW plant amidst the corporate headquarters and Vue Cinemas that occupy much of the rest of the space.

With a population of over 10,000, Blackbird Leys has been described as 'the largest council estate in Europe'. This is an implausible claim – to be larger than Gropiusstadt, the Paris *banlieue*, Marzahn or Ursynow, it'd have to be larger than Oxford itself – which mainly reflects Oxford's excessive belief in its own centrality; but the estate is definitely comparable to the places mentioned above, for one very obvious reason. Blackbird Leys is a *banlieue*, perhaps the only one in England: a peripheral, single-class suburb at the edge of an overwhelmingly bourgeois city. Like Paris, and unlike, say, Leicester, East London or Birmingham, Oxford has incessantly been told how wonderful it is, and that wonderfulness is largely connected with having survived the Industrial Revolution unscathed, and hence unscathed by the presence of a working class. It did, especially from the 1910s after the foundation of Morris Cowley, acquire a classic industrial proletariat. Sooner or later, that had to be housed somewhere where the architectural and social effect would not be unsightly. Many of those who were moved to Blackbird Leys originally lived in the city centre, on the sites where the Westgate and the Oxford Ice Rink now stand. There could have been high-density housing here, like in the less 'historic' cities mentioned above; there could even have been the more conservative approach tried in Edinburgh, where traditionalist workers' housing was merged imperceptibly into the medieval fabric. Neither happened, and neither it seems was even considered.

What is Blackbird Leys like, however, as a piece of picturesque planning? That's not a facetious question. Although the need to get it done all at once means that the slow historical accretions of the High were impossible, the estate is very much an example of the 'picturesque', Festival of Britain-influenced moment in English modernism. There are no straight lines in the town plan, only winding streets, cul-de-sacs, even a proper Crescent. The two tower blocks seem mainly to be there for the same kind of vertical punctuation as the Gothic and baroque spires of the High, a way of injecting visual interest into what would otherwise be a pretty faceless low-rise sprawl. There's no bare concrete, and most of the housing – even, towers aside, the flats – has pitched roofs. There's a subtle use of colour, with terraces, semis and blocks of various sizes clad in rich dark weatherboarding or with pretty, crisp yellow and green spandrels to their windows. The scale of the blocks is often mixed up: from one spot there's a view of a single-storey terrace and a three-storey block of flats with red tiles and balconies, with one of the towers sandwiched between. These sort of juxtapositions were obviously not accidental, but part of a plan. The spaces in between are badly maintained, with most of the blocks of flats (indeed most of what hasn't been snapped up with Right to Buy) left stained and dilapidated, but in and of themselves they're usually well-considered, with a lot of trees, a lot of green space, a lot of places where children could play, and where it could be pleasant to walk. So, other than the near-total lack of upkeep, why does Blackbird Leys feel so sad?

The decision to build a *banlieue* rather than inner-city estates meant that Oxford's architects had to design something resembling a small New Town. It suffers from the defects of most new towns, largely a fixation with keeping densities low and distances high, in order to avoid any suspicion of resembling the dense urban slums thrown up by the Industrial Revolution. All those green verges look quite nice, but they make the area feel suburban and wan, as does the street plan, endlessly winding and looping back on itself. These are not recipes for social breakdown or even mild ennui, as plenty of well-maintained low-density estates can attest. The problem is that given the uncertainty as to whether Blackbird Leys is a suburb, a new town or anything in particular, it has no centre. There's a sports hall, schools, a pub, a shopping parade, and not too far away the joys of Templars Square and myriad retail parks, but in terms of real amenity and activity, pickings are slim indeed. The estate used to have a rep for joyriding, and it's not terribly hard to see why. But lots of the frustrations and absences in Blackbird Leys must be a direct consequence of its role as a great container for the working class in Oxford. The people of Blackbird Leys themselves are fully aware of this.

Over the last few years they have elected councillors from the Independent Working Class Association, an outgrowth of anti-fascist street fighters Red Action which seems almost entirely localized in Blackbird Leys. Their politics are based on the concerns of working-class 'communities' in some unexpected ways. IWCA policies include organizing demonstrations against local drug dealers, community-based crackdowns on anti-social behaviour, and campaigning for the social facilities so conspicuously wanting in Blackbird Leys. Crime and the 'student left' are its great adversaries.[12] Interestingly, they never have a presence on national demonstrations, barely exist on the Internet, and have received little press coverage or presence. They just build up their base in beleaguered working-class areas, seemingly regardless of the means chosen to achieve it. A sort of Independent Labour Party without the Christianity and the trade unionism, and without much socialism; but holding fast to the truth that the working class has no political representation in the twenty-first century, and that the consequences of this are dire. If anyone doubts it, put them on a number 5 bus and get them to look out of the window.

Chapter Eleven

Leicester: Another Middle England

Floating in Space

Get on a bus in the centre of Leicester, and a fifteen-minute drive will take you to a place which conveys the argument of this book better than any other. Ask the driver to tell you when the bus arrives at the National Space Centre. The route goes through a pleasingly grand-scaled Midland city that is suddenly smashed to pieces by a vast flyover and becomes straggling suburbia at great speed, with semis and large red-brick factories scattered by wide roads. In the distance you will be able to see a blue, bubble-shaped tower. Get off here. Now, you're not far from the centre of town, but you're still in a suburbia which could conceivably go on like this for miles. Nicely proportioned council red-brick semis, lumpier private semis with big bay windows, tall chimneys in the near distance. The commingling of (mostly disused) indus-try with suburbia makes clear that this is the Midlands, not the North. Walk towards the bubble tower, and the semis are abruptly replaced with tight rows of terraces. Then turn past warehouses and metal sheds into the tellingly-named Exploration Drive, and have a good boggle.

The National Space Centre was built in 2001 to a design by Sir Nicholas Grimshaw, a 'high-tech' architect whose speciality is the application of light cladding to thin, tensile structures, an aesthetic that wants at once to be disposable and environmentally friendly. Grimshaw also designed what is probably the recent modern building most loved by the public at large, the Eden

Project in Cornwall, a *Silent Running*-cum-Buckminster Fuller experiment that is, helpfully, on a reservation in the country-side and hence removed from the everyday. The National Space Centre, as its surroundings make clear, is in as everyday a loca-tion as could be imagined, and by unassumingly placing space exploration in such a location, the Centre's sponsors and design-ers were continuing some kind of modernist project of inserting the extraordinary and strange into the quotidian. It's fun to see a sign pointing you to space next to a completely mundane row of terraced houses. It's also fun to see this bizarre, bulbous crea-tion looming out from behind them. This might or might not be making the place unpopular. At any rate, the local nickname for the place is apparently the rather deflating 'the Maggot'.

The Maggot's towering size is dictated by its contents. There is a permanent exhibition on the space race and our continuing, if relatively paltry attempts to explore beyond our own planet – something that was dead topical in 2011, fifty years after Yuri Gagarin. You have to pay for the permanent exhibition, but help-fully, the most interesting exhibits for those who don't have much interest in interactive advertainment or those who aren't here with children are entirely public, just at the entrance to the Centre's café, so you can see them without paying a penny. Next to the place where you can get your fizzy drink is a Soyuz spacecraft, the only one on show to the public in Western Europe. The hammer and sickle and 'SSSR' are proudly displayed on the hull. The bubble-like shape was evidently an inspiration for the exterior, and how wonderful it is that Leicester has a tower based on the design of a Soyuz module! The module itself looks like it might have been a bit more claustrophobic, but nonetheless. Then, look up from here, and two rockets take up the tower's multi-storey height; a Blue Streak missile, raw and banal, and an American Thor missile, which like the Soyuz was more 'designed'. It's strange to be admiring the design of nuclear missiles, but apt, as therein lies the central contradiction in enthusiasm for the space race.

Apt also is the area around the National Space Centre. The Centre was lottery-funded, part of some overarching regen-eration 'offer', but as so often it seems to have stalled half-way through. The spectacular, signature museum is there, it got built, and here at least it's quite delightful. Very close to it, housing got built. Of what sort? A sign tells all. 'Abbey Meadows West' promises 'high-quality traditional housing', along with 'executive luxury housing' and a 'car showroom (pre-sold to Audi)'. That high-quality traditional housing is not traditional in form, since that would involve coherent streets, a regular layout, maybe even a grid plan; but it is traditional in aesthetic, in that each house is built from load-bearing brick, with a tiled roof. This series of cul-de-sacs within cul-de-sacs with abundant car parking and security features belongs to a tradition that dates back all the way to 1920s Southern California. It's as twentieth-century as a Soyuz spaceship. Nonetheless, the signifiers, which are important, are all telling you that this is your home, Englishman, and hence also your castle. Even the computer renders on the billboards have a faint misty patina to them, to make it all look extra wistful and dreamy. They're the product of volume housebuilders Bellway, who have a nice line in creepy advertisements. A mother and baby, with gleaming white skin of positively nuclear radiance. The advertisement is encouraging you to customize your home, with 'Bespoke Additions'.

These are the two poles. The executive, traditionalist estate, and the lottery-funded Space Centre. The time of the latter is over, the time of the former is now returning. In between is the part that neither New Labour nor the Tories have shown much interest in – industry, research and development, science. There are derelict factories nearby, their roofs smashed up to ensure that they can't be re-used. Then there's a massive stretch of overgrown scrubland, with another large sign announcing the Leicester Science Park, 'circa 3000 sq m of innovation business space'. Apparently it was supposed to commence in summer 2010, but in July 2011 there was no sign of any work on the site whatsoever. There's only wasteland separating the two forms of redevelopment. In between them is a story that is seldom told, where high-tech architects like Nicholas Grimshaw thought that they could mass-produce modernist housing on what Buckminster Fuller called 'spaceship earth', a form of housing as perfectly tailored to function and need, and as unashamed about technology and modernity, as spacecraft. What happened instead was that volume housebuilders took up the mantle of mass production and created simulations of the old world, cranked and twisted so that all living space would be tailored to that other mass-produced, modern object, the car. So the outcome was that those high-tech architects designed special, upmarket, expensive cultural buildings, in which you could detect some faint trace of their earlier dreams of a total revolution in earthly space.

Up Against Orton Square

I purchased a return on the bus to the National Space Centre from Leicester Railway Station. I got on the same number bus to get back, but was told I couldn't use my return, despite the fact it was the same line, because *this* bus was run by a different operating company. If there's a better argument for the renationalization of our ridiculous, deregulated public transport than this, I haven't heard it. But get off that bus, after you've finished seething, and you'll find that Leicester is about as good as a medium-sized English city gets, with all of the best features and relatively few of its mistakes and frustrations, at least inside the ring road. Leicester has the highest non-white population of any British city outside London, and seems as unassuming about this as about everything else – and given that it doesn't have Birmingham's vastness and mass, or its status as 'Second City', its occasional provincialisms are much less infuriating. It has lots of the best things about northern cities – refusal of Good Taste, proper urban scale and civic pride, a great big covered market – without their tendency to blow their own trumpets with vehemence. It has far greater density of interesting twentieth- and twenty-first-century architecture than Birmingham, and can also lay claim to a couple of the most important modern buildings of the last hundred years. It doesn't trumpet this either, although perhaps it should. Nonetheless, if Leicester is mediocre, then there is some hope that we might be able to discover a decent, worthwhile mediocrity in English urbanism, rather than a lumpen, thuggish mediocrity.

First you have to get over a miserable prospect around the railway station. Hulking red-brick offices for the likes of KPMG are detailed with lots of little pitched roofs and banded brickwork in an invariably inept attempt to convince you that they are not, in fact, stodgy, identikit and obnoxious but fabulously dynamic and contextual additions to the townscape. A dual carriageway runs inbetween. This feels like the banker belt on the Leeds ring road, or worse, Reading, but it's deceptive, and soon you find yourself in a bustling town centre, particularly rich in tasteless Victorian Grand Hotels, soft-porn Victorian monuments (check out 'Grief', near the Town Hall) and in fine early-twentieth-century architecture, usually at some midway point between the floridity of art nouveau and the more rectilinear grace of art deco. The Fenwick's store, part-glazed, with twisty iron balconies, is one case in point; another is the extremely strange Singer building, a long range with a barrel-vaulted glass roof, Egyptian columns, and various forms of Imperialist decorative dressing, from majolica ships and Union Jack panels to allegorical representations of the subject territories of Black Africa, Egypt, Burma and India. It was designed in 1904, during the Twilight of Empire, by one Arthur Wakerley, architect, Whig, and Mayor of Leicester. Many of Leicester's current residents would be right to regard this building with the same horror that many Varsovians reserve for Stalin's Palace of Culture and Science – an unaltered monument to imperial dominance and barbarism – but nobody seems bothered, and at the moment the structure is subdivided into a fitness centre, a karate school, a caff, a kebab shop and a nail parlour with an imperial transition encapsulated in its name, 'USA Nails'. The area around is pedestrianized, lined by skinny trees. Nearby is the similarly individual stone and glass tower of Lewis's department store, and several very enjoyably silly commercial buildings. Evidently, in Leicester, the fact that nobody was looking meant not third-rate copying of metropolitan models, but the welcome refusal of metropolitan good taste.

The ensemble that gives the best view of the pleasures of Leicester is, rather unexpectedly, a Cultural Quarter, centred on a square named after Joe Orton, the working-class queer playwright, who harboured very little affection for his birthplace (though what he might have thought of it now is an open question). It would be nice if, in light of many of the stranger

Leicester buildings, it was possible to point to an unbroken local tradition of peculiar and imaginative architecture, but instead, as usual, an icon provider was parachuted in. For once, though, the urban structure was so strong that the iconist – Uruguayan designer Rafael Vinoly – conformed to it rather than ignoring it. The area has a centrifugal, spiralling force which is exacerbated rather than broken by Vinoly's Curve Theatre, a sweeping, but relatively simple and undemonstrative design from an architect more usually inclined to the showily egotistical. It's perhaps a storey or so too tall, but it takes up well a rhythm that begins with the staggered, stepped curtain wall of a post-war office building, veering towards a Weimaresque Odeon cinema by Harry Weedon and then continuing down Rutland Street, where there is a cluster of fascinating ex-industrial buildings. In the other corner, a Serbian Orthodox church sits behind its churchyard. The industrial buildings of Rutland Street are well worth an exploration in themselves. One is an early 1920s replica of the Philadelphia Headquarters of the Pfister and Vogel leather company, boasting green tiles, wide, cubistic bay windows and art nouveau carvings. Terracotta warehouses just opposite make for a less strange, but still powerful and intriguing townscape. Inevitably, a couple have been turned into luxury living solutions, but as Cultural Quarters go, this is significantly less dumb than most.

Markets, Marketing and Ornament

The Northernness of this Midland city can be gleaned from its vast complex of street markets, which introduces a welcome note of chaos and bustle and a working-class presence into a city which, you soon find, has tried to stake as much on big retail as everywhere else. Walking round Leicester's market, you ask yourself how long this place can possibly last – how long it will be allowed to occupy space which could so much more profitably be operated by mall developers like Hammersons or LendLease. There are really several markets, one enormous, practically medieval covered market that has escaped from fourteenth-century Flanders, and a red-brick, modernist affair, also covered, with complex multiple layers inside. It all manages to slant the city centre into something a great deal more genuinely lively, less segregated and tight-arsed, than its equivalents in more *dirigiste*, developer-centred cities such as Birmingham. You can find second-hand bookshops here of a quality more common in Glasgow and London, and that's a reason to cheer loudly. Not that Leicester doesn't share the country-wide belief that a huge John Lewis and lots of car parking are the answer to industrial decline, but here, again rather surprisingly, the results have been treated, sometimes, with a degree of architectural seriousness. So there is a lot of shopping, but in some compelling, if problematic, buildings.

Most interesting is the Haymarket Centre, an early 1970s scheme by BDP in their vigorous, red-brick, socialist prime. The façades of the shopping centre and the car park are deceptively simple, long rectilinear stretches of sleek red brickwork, with a hint of 1920s Dutch Modernism. So far, so much like a superior, but nonetheless functionally similar post-war mall, a slab of 'comprehensive redevelopment'. Yet on the other side it resolves into a different building entirely. The stair towers become sharp corner compositions, and the brick range extends into tall, thin pillars. The angular geometry of a stairway to an upper storey emerges at one end, a cantilevered block at another, while shops and cafés take up the ground floor, backing away to form a public square. A constructivist sculpture by Hubert Dalwood, a slightly anthropomorphic alignment of metal panels, occupies part of the square. This is the point where the Haymarket Centre becomes the Haymarket Theatre, an extremely unusual mixed usage for its period. It's a great building, fitting in with the general sense of doing very clever and unusual things in an unassuming, relaxed way. It also has the feeling of being severely down-at-heel, a location for loitering and street drinking, although that's better than the ruthless cleansing of such activities that would take place in the Business Improvement District of Birmingham. The reason for its slight sadness is that the Theatre itself has moved lock, stock and barrel to the Cultural Quarter, to the new shiny regeneration theatre. Evidently a city of 300,000 couldn't accommodate *two* theatres. It's interesting that culture now has to be zoned, put in a reservation, rather than placed in the centre of the everyday. At the time of writing, it has been standing abandoned for five years.

Walk through here and you find that the city has managed to create a bustling, pedestrianized centre without the same sense of yuppie reservation as many similar cities, although perhaps that's not for want of trying. The unusually decent architecture extends even to that grimmest of styles – '80s vernacular – as where a white weatherboarded clock tower en piloti marks an entrance to a little simulation of medieval bustle, and manages to pull it off. Like the Haymarket Theatre, it's very red-brick and very Midlands. The inverse approach to this is the Highcross Centre, Leicester's big-bucks, money-spinning megamall, the one with a big John Lewis in it, the one that necessitates the big horrible ring road to convey suburban shoppers into it. Here, developers Hammerson brought in another firm of signature architects, the Koolhaas-trained Foreign Office Architects, who were in the early 2000s considered faintly avant-garde, unlike the usual shopping mall grunts such as Chapman Taylor or Benoy. However, Hammerson's choice had a certain logic to it. They hadn't just picked them out because they liked an iconic building they saw in the papers. FOA (who split a couple of years ago due to the break-up of the extra-professional partnership of the two lead architects, Farshid Moussavi and Alejandro Zaera-Polo) were enthusiasts for ornament and cladding, and the concentration of architectural energies on the dressing of façades; Moussavi wrote a treatise on ornament, a strikingly non-modernist move. FOA's use of ornament was not traditionalist, in the clumsy '80s post-modernist fashion, but heavily theorized and non-referential. The point remains, though, that they were architects who would let the mall's developers do pretty much whatever they liked with the shopping centre typology, with its vast eating of space, its enclosed, air-conditioned interiors and its abundant car parking, and would then model the result in an attractive, and reliably 'iconic', way. It's the architectural equivalent to our economic hurtle back to the nineteenth century, where the architect provided a tectonic frock for engineering.

FOA's section of Highcross – a vast structure based on continuous accretions, one of several similarities between malls and cathedrals – is Shire West, at the mall's northern edge. A standard double-height space is slightly 'humanized' via top-lighting and a bit of wood, but a bridge to the John Lewis marks the real join. This bridge is a buckle of inclined steel, leading to a very large glass box dressed in a flowing, organic pattern, apparently taken from one of John Lewis's old catalogues. Arts and Crafts, but with all that pesky stuff about the dignity of labour taken out. It is, undoubtedly, a little more aesthetically interesting than the average mall, especially from the street, where that dashing bridge glistens into the department-store box; but it still feels like an abdication from architecture's other role as something that consciously encloses and creates space and location. It's always sad and funny, when Fabians and (non-neo) Liberals talk of creating an employee-owned 'John Lewis capitalism', to recall the vicious damage that John Lewis have perpetrated upon British cities over the last two decades, their prestigious presence always necessitating overwhelming, car-centred retail hangars, usually as part of shopping malls. Not all of FOA's intervention is the department store, though – there's also a multiplex cinema. This is usually a windowless, big-shed typology, and FOA of course don't try to change that – instead, they cast the box in shining zinc panels. Silvery metal is a much more predictable form of Urban Regen architecture, and as with the John Lewis, the effect is aspirational in a slightly fur-coat-and-no-knickers way, and equally tacky-exciting. Then, if you get back onto street level, you find yourself in a more mundane area of the 'Highcross Quarter', wood and brick-clad buildings lining public squares. While the market pulses with life, this place sits completely empty on a bright July afternoon, the bottles of ketchup and the glass pepper grinders left lonely on the outside tables.

'Elite, not elitist'

Leicester University is not a member of the Russell Group, the elite cabal that dominates the university system and which now has the right to set astonishingly high fees, but it's one of the most successful universities not to be part of it. Unlike the other colleges in industrial towns in this book – the University of Teesside, say, or the University of Plymouth – Leicester's University is well aware of its power and prestige. To reach it, I walked from the dual carriageway onto a little square, with a hilariously vulgar statue of a Victorian notable, the dissenting minister and writer Robert Hall. His robust figure raises a hand, into which (surely) a student has inserted a crushed beer can and a dangling binbag. A more multicultural monument stands next to him, a rare permanent homage to Leicester's impressive diversity – the word 'tranquillity' translated into German, Welsh and Urdu, amongst others. Victoria Park takes up a wide stretch of this area, an amenity centred around a puzzling, severe First World War monument designed by Edwin Lutyens, an uncanny presence, using the classical language with what was even then an unusual lack of cliché. There's a close of Arts and Crafts cottages next to a fire station, strictly private property, but worth a peek.

As you walk around admiring all this, however, you're desperately trying to avoid looking at a much larger structure – Opal Court, a clustered tower of student housing. Like many towers of student housing, it is erected from prefabricated modules. This is not always a route to a horrible building, but it is when the architects – here, Stephen George & Partners – stretch every sinew

to stop that modularity and regularity from becoming visible
on the façade, which is important so that the students' parents
don't think they're sending their kids to live in a tower block.
The whole 2000s panoply was thrown at it – a stepped, irregular
skyline, thin stock-brick cladding, blue plastic cladding, 'high-
tech' struts protruding at random, and several of those wavy
roofs – in the attempt to hide the sheer bloody size of the thing.
At its full stretch, it's twenty-three bays wide and sixteen storeys
high – an enormous building. The only way to design something
of this mass and to make it viable is to accept that you've built a
gigantic block, rather than this ridiculous fudge. It's one of the
first things you see on the train into Leicester, which is deeply
unfair to the city. In the years just before the crash, several of
these (none quite so appalling, but near enough) appeared around
Leicester, as if in a bid to offset whatever efforts at coherence and
thoughtfulness it had made in the centre.

So the best thing to do at this point is go straight into the
University, and look at three buildings which, whatever else can
be said about them, are towers that were closely pondered, con-
ceived from start to finish as entities that could be seen for miles,
and which hence had to offer something other than patronizing
platitudes or monolithic blandness to the eye. These three towers
can be seen from Victoria Park, where they suggest a tiny modernist city of greater design interest than most actual cities. They
are the Charles Wilson building, designed by Denys Lasdun; the
Attenborough Tower, by Arup; and the Engineering Building, by
James Stirling and James Gowan. The Charles Wilson building,
built in 1963, houses various bits and bobs from common rooms
to cafés. Like all three of these towers, it's complex, its different parts articulated and emphasized, but not as in the artificial
cladding of Blair hats and slatted wood: the articulation springs
from the inside of the building, grows out of its internal forces.
The Charles Wilson building has six lower-rise floors that are
wide and stark, then a thinner tower, with a sculptural fire escape
placed at a corner – probably more to create a constructivist dash
than to facilitate easy escape from fire. It's as ornamental as the
John Lewis, perhaps, but how much more tectonically vigorous
and powerful! It has the wilful sculptural play of a Frank Lloyd

Wright conveyed through a more dour, northern sensibility, in well-detailed, smooth brown concrete. The 1969 Attenborough Tower, for the Arts and Humanities Department, rises from a long and low podium up to eighteen storeys. It's prefabricated, a simple matter of precast concrete modules, subtly curved, with dozens of identical windows, at an incline from top to bottom. It doesn't hide its height, it doesn't hide its method of construction, and it feels far more humane as a statement – its shape distinctive and attractive, futuristic and slightly kitsch, with zoom curves and angles. So the walk from Opal Court to here is a good place to convert doubters of the rightness in the modernist cause; but at the centre of it all is a building which is often considered to have broken apart all the certainties and theories of modernism as it had been practised until then.

Stirling and Gowan's Engineering Building is a banner for an Anglicized modernism that horrified Nikolaus Pevsner, one which drew on constructivism, expressionism, and the baleful, twisted forms of the industrial revolution. It's several weird and angular little things, crammed onto a tiny site, a glazed engineering block and a tower put through all kinds of cantilevers, twists and turns in order to use its space. As anyone interested in twentieth-century architecture will know, it forms an enduringly photogenic ensemble, the tower rising sleek, on skinny concrete stilts, above a cantilevered lecture theatre; a series of sculptural shapes clad in mass-produced red tiles, above a red-brick base. Unlike much of what had gone before it, the Engineering Building did not sweep up its functions into a clear, transparent envelope, but splayed them out crankily and gawkily, mocking the Apollonian rationalism of 'High Modernism' as it went. In photographs, like all Stirling's 'red' buildings, it crackles with electricity, but what is peculiar about the Engineering Building is that, unlike many of its antecedents, it doesn't have much in the way of physical presence. Unlike the heavy concrete Brutalism of late Le Corbusier, or of followers such as Denys Lasdun, the materials are lightweight, deliberately so.

The tiles have none of the physical heft of the red brick that they evoke from a distance. Rather than overwhelm, or carry you along with it, the Engineering Building encourages the same sort

of rapt, fascinated, but essentially cold gaze you might direct at the intricacies of a Swiss watch, a clockwork toy, a Geometric drawing, or a Van Doesburg painting. As much as the work of Lutyens, helpfully just round the corner, it's an architecture of allusion, paradox and puzzlement. There are so many possible angles, views and positions, all of which show something surprising and strange: under the lecture theatre, looking towards the smaller of the two towers, with its thin, louvred windows broken up by a curved red mass; the engineering laboratories from round the back, when their faceted, diagonally placed diamonds peek out above nondescript neo-Georgian buildings; under the stilts of the taller tower, where a glass tube contains an exterior staircase; from a distance, where you can survey the whole ensemble. All this has been extensively documented and photographed in dozens of books, yet it still feels like a surprise to discover in Leicester, even in a University this pleased with itself. It could be argued that the work ended an architecture of physicality and replaced it with an architecture of built theory, which has had certain dire consequences – but if so, what a magnificent dead end this is.

This superb mini-city has its lower-rise buildings, most of a high quality, across podiums and walkways, but there's something that rankles, and it's made explicit by the banners of the University, those adverts fluttering in the wind. 'Ranked in the top 2% of Universities worldwide'; 'Elite, not Elitist'. The latter is one of the pithiest statements of neoliberal English cultural ideology I've ever heard. Elite? Of course it's Elite, we're obviously a ruling class. But we're not Elitist. We're just the same as you, and hey, we probably had the same opportunities as you, but you just didn't take them. We won't ever suggest we're better or smarter than you, and good God, we certainly won't try and bring you culture, or knowledge. That would be awfully patronizing of us. We'll rule over you, but we won't be overbearing, or least of all, paternalistic about it. There's a consequence to this, and that's the stretch of wasteland in between the National Space Centre and the Abbey Meadows housing, where all that research and development was supposed to meet working-class Leicester. The contrast between the Space Centre and the neo-Georgian rabbit hutches, too, is a consequence. We'll explore space, you'll live in the eighteenth century, with better car parking.

Chapter Twelve

Lincoln: Between Two Cathedrals

A Googie Tent in Ermine

As has already been implied, there exists a different kind of 'city' in the UK from those catalogued in this book. The Cathedral City is an entirely different genre, and one which I'm trying to avoid. Not because they're uninteresting – the panoramic view of Winchester from St Catherine's Hill is not to be sniffed at, however self-satisfied it might be down below – but because they don't need the extra attention. Nobody needs convincing of their merits. Excepting the handful of former Cathedral Cities that have accommodated later development and become modern conurbations – Bristol, London, Glasgow – they are a pleasant but over-favoured adjunct to the places where most of us actually live. They have largely stayed within or nearly within their medieval walls or been wound into the tightest of green belts, becoming packed with cottagey retail and branches of the curious mock-antique chain store Past Times. They're places to visit, not places to live, unless you're either lucky or a venture capitalist. Lincoln, you learn after a couple of hours walking here, is interesting because it fits neither model. It isn't a Wen that still retains a Cathedral in the middle of it somewhere, like Bristol, and it isn't an inhabited museum piece, like Canterbury. In fact, Lincoln has some qualities that are lacking in most British cities. It's something of a well-kept secret, a medium-sized industrial town that didn't barbarize its built environment, a Cathedral City that excelled in post-war modernist architecture.

Walking round it entails having your preconceptions knocked down, one by one.

I wasn't in Lincoln to write about it, but to attend a conference on the history and aesthetics of council housing, which took place in the Christian educational institution Bishop Grosseteste College, just next to the Ermine Estate – a very large public housing project mostly built between 1952 and 1958. One of the organizers had grown up here; in the course of the event it was an eye-opener to find so many modernist enthusiasts and concrete fetishists who had grown up in places like this. The reason why the conference was here, by the Ermine Estate, was partly because the place is a very typical example of its kind, but also because of the building at its heart. The culmination of the event was a visit to St John the Baptist, a 1963 church by a local architect, Sam Scorer. Around it the estate twists its winding roads, and various different eras in social democratic design can be picked out and compared. The main shopping parade is 'Festival style', the jolly, ornamented modernism that emerged out of the 1951 Festival of Britain, as seen at the Lansbury Estate in Poplar – a curved block with little bow windows that evoke a fishing village or a seaside town, a curious sight after the featureless steppe of the nearby Lincolnshire countryside. The houses and flats are all uncontroversial but decent, often with well-trimmed and maintained public greenery around; the streets were covered in blossom on the day I visited. There's an elegant little public library right in the centre of the place, with its rooms at jagged angles to pick up light. I have seen very few council estates in such good condition, but that doesn't prepare one for the sight of St John the Baptist. The estate is determinedly mild and moderate, far from the avant-garde; its parish church is quite the opposite.

St John the Baptist is a Googie building. This architectural genre, begun by the Californian architect John Lautner in the late 1940s, is modernism on the razzle, a completely anti-functionalist play of swooping engineering, space-age ornamentation and the aesthetically productive futurist illusion that a static building is a moving, active thing. Sam Scorer was from an affluent Lincolnshire family, and yet there are few modernist buildings in working-class areas so completely devoid of condescension.

This building is a matter of pure pleasure, unrestrained delight, play for the senses. The exterior is grey, which at least conforms slightly more to austere type, but what the eye notices is the form, the way that the hyperbolic paraboloid roof plunges down and up the glass and concrete walls. From the outside, it's a curio; inside, it's a masterpiece, completely out on its own in the UK. That roof is detailed in delicate stretches of wood, miming an 'upturned ark' effect that may not be entirely intended. The pews run in a semi-circle round the altar, feeling tightly packed and warm, but also very small – the church commissioners of the early 1960s were evidently taking a realistic view of likely attendances. The architectural form embraces striking artistic interventions.

The sculptures and fittings are modernist: a concrete altar, a semi-abstract crushed steel Roman centurion by Charles Edward Sansbury standing guard over the crucifixion, deep red plush benches just behind, and a buckled, skinny cross that evokes Giacometti. But at first you don't notice any of this – it's the space around the altar itself which simply astonishes. The coloured glass of the vast window, by Keith New, is loud and bright. It claims to represent, in a non-representational way, 'the Revelation of God's Plan for Man's Redemption', but that wild agglomeration of colour and shape has no hint of determinism. What it conveys is a complex but unmediated sense of joy, as your eye runs over a series of brash scarlets, greens, yellows and blues. The church's unusually useful guide tells you that 'the central section, dominated by a large crimson shape, represents the Holy Trinity', and 'the shape on the right with a largely green background represents the nativity of Christ'. As with a piece of conceptual art, the 'intention' is only obvious if you read a guide, if someone's telling you what to see, but it doesn't matter in the slightest – a 'plan' is visible, as is 'redemption', and the theology behind it is unclear enough to be ignored by the non-believer of whatever stripe. The absence of any darkness, any crepuscular gloom, any images of pain or tribulation, makes this a church that seemingly has no fetish for suffering – at least until you look more closely at the smaller fittings, more 'normal' christs and virgins donated by parishioners. Atheists longing for the warmth and ritual of religion could console themselves with the thought that St John the

Baptist's conveys a civic joy, a pleasure in architectural form and assembled community, that doesn't *necessarily* require religious belief.

From the Steep Hill to Siemens

There is a more famous religious building in Lincoln. After a journey through streets of affluent, leafy villas, the Cathedral Square is choked by traffic, mostly very large vehicles – not an encouraging sign. The houses on the square are perhaps excessively pretty, restored to within an inch of their lives, but the Cathedral itself is furious, undeniable. I approached it from the back, admiring the monsters and the superbly inhuman scale of the buttresses. The front façade is of similarly outrageous proportions, and inside, it's impossible not to gasp. They knew what they were doing. Walking round the aisles, I noticed sat on the pews several architects and historians who had been at the conference on council estates. This is not nearly as peculiar as it may at first appear. Modernism, at its extremes, on its Brutalist or expressionist edges, is an architecture of outlandish scale, capacious vaults, audacious structural engineering, stark games with length and repetition, light and shade, a willingness to court absurdity, and, frankly, a tendency to the frightening and sublime. Regularity, neatness, order and 'context' were to be shunned, as the assumption – as with, say, Park Hill in Sheffield – was that this would be the city's peak, the *Stadtkrone*, the pivotal monument for the entire area, visible for miles. Here, with similar autonomy and excess, the glory and fear of God was the object, however much you might today admire this place as the embodiment of human potential, and feel elated and uplifted by the engineering, care and craftsmanship rather than the devotion. The question that could be posed at Brutalism was perhaps: who was frightened, and who was doing the frightening? Obviously, much in Lincoln Cathedral is admirable for wholly un-Brutalist qualities such as intricate ornament, and I lack the language or belief to truly understand this structure, to do it any real justice, to be much other than awed by it. Undoubtedly it is, however, the centre of a topographical masterpiece.

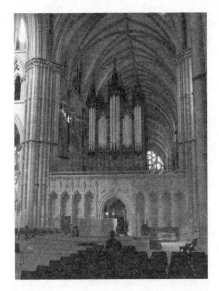

When you look out of the gateways that lead to the Cathedral, you can see bulging, leaning non-mock Tudor, cobbles and tea shops. At the junction with Castle Hill begins the usefully named Steep Hill, thoroughly restored and cutesified. But although there's an enormous amount of architectural (and not merely archaeological) interest in these medieval, Tudor and Georgian houses tumbling down the slope, it's the slow transition that starts here that is especially unusual and compelling. Already from Steep Hill you can see long industrial sheds in the distance, across the flatlands; but as you descend from here to the main shopping street, you find that this gorgeous chocolate-box Lincoln has shifted, at first almost imperceptibly and then decisively, into a small but confident East Midlands industrial town. There are Victorian buildings, with wide expanses of glass and terracotta ornament, and there are post-war modernist buildings of an unexpected tact and conviction. There are tasteless 1980s postmodernist shopping centres, there is kitschy Blairite public art, and there are residential tower blocks in the near distance. Traces of Lincoln's previous existence are thrilling when interleaved with this mundane melange. The inhabited sixteenth-century High Bridge is a timber-framed block, clearly wilting with its own weight. Walk up a tiny stairway next to it, and you find yourself in somewhere roughly functionalist, with what looks like a Victorian warehouse and the back-end of a mall abutting the Bridge and the waterway beneath.

The other route along the river Witham foregrounds the aforementioned Blairite sculpture, a ridiculous 2002 piece entitled 'Empowerment' (of course it is!), in which two steel figures tumble towards each other in a manner evoking now-forgotten early '90s cybersex film *The Lawnmower Man*. It was designed by one Stephen Broadbent and funded by the local Siemens factory, an unusually direct example of industrial patronage. Further down this long high street, there is the Market, the neoclassical portico of the Corn Exchange, and next to this two modern buildings. One is a quasi-Brutalist block, all rough concrete and red brick, the other a Miesian smoked-glass bank of patrician elegance. Both have the exact same scale as the earlier buildings, but make no concessions to 'in keeping'. Other towns such as Bristol, much larger and much richer than Lincoln, so often lack this unassuming kind of modernism; perhaps because talent cost money, or because it went unrecognized, or perhaps because there was simply less talent locally; or simply because Lincoln's ruling class actually *liked* their city. It later transpires that the Miesian bank is another Sam Scorer building – similarly American in derivation, but otherwise most unlike St John the Baptist's glorious display. The style for the job. Right at the end of the high street, where it meets the dual carriageway and railway station, the change is complete. The blue sheds of the Siemens works, a concrete viaduct and the intense red brick of the Bus Station are the monuments of a completely different city to that of Steep Hill – a ragged-arsed Midlands engineering town that could never adorn a postcard or a biscuit tin. Yet the transition between the two has been gradual and careful, and the city stayed coherent. It's a class city, like any other – but somehow the contradictions have been managed, smoothed over, and the city somehow retained its self-worth. This is no small thing.

The University of Lincoln (on Strike)

Brayford Pool, the city's old docks, is where much new development has been centred in recent years, following the reliable rule that an urban waterway means Old Corruption can't be too far away. There is much in the way of 'stunning developments', and here also is the only really awful building I saw in Lincoln (this is not faint praise, as most cities this size have several dozen): a grim exurban Odeon multiplex. It's huge, and destructive, and it's especially terrible because here at Brayford Pool is where you turn around and take in the view of the city, and realize its full magnificence – the Cathedral and the Castle erupting out of the landscape like rock formations. Even here, though, there has been some intelligence – fast-food chains Nando's and Prezzo are in another Sam Scorer structure, once more showing the architect in his Googie moment, with another hyperbolic paraboloid roof, but this time thinner, more of a self-display. It was built as a car showroom, then became – oh yes – a library, before reaching its current terminus serving foodstuffs. This is a lively embankment, and the reason for this is soon apparent – the University of Lincoln has its new campus here.

This is also the reason for some drably generic student flats, but the presence of an inner-city university may help explain exactly why Lincoln feels peculiarly optimistic. The University buildings are nothing to shout about, neomodernism of a reasonably inoffensive stamp – rendered concrete, a few dashes of blocky colour, tacked-on aluminium for the walkways – but there is much, much worse elsewhere. They're also deathly quiet, considering the proximity of the dining and drinking on the other side of the Pool. This is because of the one-day strike affecting the Universities. Bishop Grosseteste College, run by the church, is shielded from the cuts, but the organizers of the council-housing conference asked for and got official UCU permission to run it, entirely due to its subject matter. The emptiness of the University itself suggests the strike has been solid.

Nonetheless, this sudden quietness is interesting. Given the enormous hike in tuition fees, the shot in the arm the University has evidently given the city may turn out to be brief. It was one of the possible explanations for why Lincoln feels, almost, in topographers Adrian Jones and Chris Matthews' words, to be a 'success story'. I didn't set out to write about Lincoln. The favourable impression the city made on me had nothing to do with two reportedly excellent new buildings, The Collection by Panter Hudspith and Bauman Lyons's The Terrace, as I didn't know they were there. I hadn't even realized there was a castle until I'd seen it in the distance. Lincoln isn't perfect – the malls and public art are poor, and the public transport is very poor indeed, something that is sure to be radically exacerbated if, as planned, the bus station is demolished and replaced with another mall. Its industries are not what they were, so it's likely that Lincoln has many of the same problems and inequalities as anywhere else in the UK, although it hides them better than most. But on the way back from Lincoln, I was mainly wondering how it had managed to be as good as it is. An expression of the paternalism of the bourgeoisie uphill towards the workers downhill? A consequence of the geographical position, away from the orgiastic speculation of the South and the please-developers-please desperation of much of the North and the West Midlands? The compact size, discouraging the 'aspirational' urge to become a 'destination'? Lying off the main lines to London? Maybe the specificity of Lincoln means it has few lessons to impart, but one of these might be – self-esteem, without self-delusion.

Chapter Thirteen

The Valleys: I Am a Pioneer,
They Call Me Primitive

Add Another Kick, Why Don't You

'South Wales needs a Plan!' declared a book published during the Great Depression, on one of the 'distressed areas' hardest hit by the 1930s. The cities of South Wales – Cardiff, Newport, Swansea – became boom towns in the late nineteenth century solely in order to export and process the produce of the coal seams that ran across the valleys; dependent on the tiny industrial towns that were hastily built to service them. This place powered the Industrial Revolution and imperial expansion more, perhaps, than any other, but that doesn't seem to have done it any favours. Now, in 2011, it seems that the Valleys need a Plan again; among the places most affected by the recession are the likes of Merthyr Tydfil, which face some of the highest rates of unemployment in the country; Merthyr is according to a report by the GMB the most difficult place to find work in the UK. The same places have been punished, in the exact same ways, yet again. The scarily ingenuous Iain Duncan Smith helpfully suggested that the people of Merthyr up sticks to Cardiff, where there are nine unemployed people for every job vacancy. The Valleys are at least topical. If the 2010s are not so much the return of the 1980s as a high-tech re-run of the 1930s, with a heavy slump and a National Government, then it makes sense that the Valleys have once more become a pejorative.

But does it make sense to include the Valleys in a book on 'Urban Britain'? They don't fit the pattern of any other rural or urban settlement in the UK. These long rows of terraces, distributed along steep, scarred and verdant hills, are obviously too dense and industrial to be 'the countryside', no matter how gorgeously they might nestle in those undulations; at the same time they're largely too bounded to feel like towns as commonly understood. They could be considered one dispersed great town, parted by billowing waves of topography. You'd have to be either very fit or very poor to attempt to negotiate it without a car, but thankfully I had a local friend who was willing. Linking the Valleys together coherently could only work via expensive, unwieldy solutions – an underground railway, a system of funiculars. Although unemployment is very high and the poverty is glaring, some moderate investment has made its way here. Since the mines were crushed in the 1980s, with the steelworks gradually following suit, call centres and local government offices filled the gap; talk of remaking them into Silicon Valleys seems to have come to little.

Self-conscious architecture, especially of the twentieth century, hasn't touched the Valleys much, although there are remarkable buildings and townscapes to be found. The Valleys are so heart-stoppingly beautiful in places that you could imagine them one day becoming tourist centres, places to get a Second Home. Tragically enough, the destruction of the area's industry has helped in this; the slag heaps have long since greened over and these man-made ridges amplify the already abundant curves and dips of the natural landscape. Snobbery is surely the main factor that checks the appearance in the *Guardian* of 'Let's move to ... Tredegar', although on some level it's their loss. What the Valleys does have is a great tradition of resistance, self-organization and militancy. Those who like to imagine that Communism was a middle-class phenomenon, fit only to be reminisced over by comedians and novelists whose parents were Party members, may need to be reminded that one of the CPGB's founding organizations was the South Wales Socialist Society, most of whose members were Syndicalist Miners. Local councils in some of these towns were left-of-labour strongholds right up until the 1980s, as with Maerdy and its Communist Mayor, Annie Powell. There are still constituencies here where the Communist

Party gets placed ahead of the Conservatives – they even have a councillor in Penderyn. Blaenau Gwent, Nye Bevan's old constituency, voted in dissident Labour candidates as MPs in the 2001 and 2005 elections, against Millbank-imposed Blairites. A local party founded from these Labourite refuseniks, Blaenau Gwent People's Voice, looked briefly as though it might be the start of something important. South Wales had, after all, done something similar before. But the imminence of a Tory government caused a return to the fold in 2010, with a huge swing to Labour; like most left-of-Labour parties (Respect, the Scottish Socialist Party), People's Voice has since disintegrated entirely. Still, at least some signs of this history should surely be visible.

London, Shanghai, Tokyo? Nope

The Valleys' geographical stretch, right through the counties of Gwent and Glamorgan, was limited by time, for us, to two county boroughs, Rhondda Cynon Taf and Blaenau Gwent, the two main concentrations, with a little addenda on Newport thrown in. That's because my gateway to the Valleys here, though not part of the Valleys proper, was Newport: a city which has a great prospect as you approach its railway station, almost like a mini-Newcastle. There's a march of bridges, from multicoloured Victorian ironwork to a couple of white-steel regen efforts, ending with a majestic, almost ethereal Transporter; to the other side, a Town Hall tower, multi-storey car parks and tall office blocks, with a ruined castle in the middle. Newport station itself has had a bit of a go at providing a suitably impressive entry point. The earlier Great Western Railway station's platforms have an advert on them illustrating a building you haven't yet met, seen from the air, with the query: 'London, Shanghai, Tokyo? Nope – Newport.' It's iconic! The building itself, designed by engineers Atkins, with some input from architect Nicholas Grimshaw, is a very mixed bag. It's a vaguely cylindrical, blob-like form, linked by sweeping pedestrian bridges, with new platform pavilions in glazed blue tiles. The detailing is horribly tinny, a PFI-standard use of cheap metals, off-the-peg railings and tacky plastics, while the circulation is needlessly complicated; but there's a germ of an idea in there to give the place some sense of arrival, at least in the circular booking hall.

It sounds trite and obvious, but the foreignness of Wales to the English eye is only really apparent when you get out of the cities and into the valley, and even more so when you're in the mountains. You slowly realize that the place's history has been formed absolutely by its topography, with the Brecon Beacons forming an impassable barrier against the raids of barbarian German tribes, and the Valleys' shapes dictating an entire pattern of settlement, after coal and ore was discovered. The hills and mountains here are captivating and strange – long, deep in their curves, with velvety contrasts of dark and light greens. The first town we come to is Aberfan, whose tightly packed terraces swarming up hillsides introduce the scene – an urban-rural landscape, of great density mingled with great swathes of green space, with precipitously settled terraces.

Normally, when you see a landscape like this, in Brecon, say, which we made a detour to later, you expect tea shops, nice restaurants, a generally genteel and slightly geriatric atmosphere. Here, you find much the same kebab and chicken shops, bookies, pubs and newsagents that you'd find in any large city, which takes a while to get used to. While Aberfan's shops might feel familiar, the landscape is anything but. Those long lines of terraces are mirrored in the linear strip of gravestones to commemorate the children killed by a landslide of coalfield waste in 1966, who were further insulted by government inaction and obstruction. It's an early warning not to romanticize the Valleys' industrial past, a reminder that any nostalgia for the mining era could be dangerously rose-tinted. These people were treated brutally by their 'superiors'; their socialism didn't come out of thin air. As the deaths in unregulated pits in late 2011 made clear, that contempt for human life hasn't changed.

The Merthyr Tydfil Café Quarter

From there, we travel to the largest of the Valleys settlements, once the largest town outright in Wales, before the ports overtook it – Merthyr Tydfil, another place full of meanings and

resonances. It has been a recent punchbag for Conservative politicians owing to its large quantity of people on benefits, including
incapacity benefits (now why on earth would an ex-mining area
have a lot of claimants for *that*?) The Red Flag, as a political
symbol, was born here, in the Merthyr Rising of 1831. It would
have been nice for this to have been commemorated in the public
art that is invariably scattered around a post-industrial town,
but there is at least a very appropriate welded metal sculpture
by Charles Sansbury (whom we have already encountered in St
John the Baptist, Lincoln) marking the entrance to the town. It's
placed on a roundabout. Sharp, severe, beautiful in its harshness,
it is very Merthyr. Opposite are offices for the Welsh Assembly:
a business-park monster, an utter architectural nullity, but surely
deeply welcome for the town itself. Next to the roundabout is
the town's only tower block. It's similarly bland as architecture,
just a big brown block, but it's notable both for being one of the
more urbes-in-rure towers in the UK, and for commanding one
of the finest views conceivable, for what is no doubt a knock-
down price. After that, we get out and have a wander around.
The poverty of the town fairly whacks you in the face, especially
in the haggard concrete shopping precinct of St Tydfil, which
feels bizarrely dense, dark and compacted for such a small town
surrounded by such lush green hills.

At least it's not entirely derelict. Walk round the residential
areas just outside the town centre, and the public buildings are in
a state of advanced decay. The Miners Hall of 1921 is a rough, late
Gothic structure that looks more like a church than a workers'
institute. Without a roof or any glass in the windows, overtaken
by greenery, it's a sad spectacle indeed. Just round the corner is
an actual church, the 1901 Unitarian, which is slotted into a line
of terraces, with an entrance arcade level with the houses' doorways and the rest slightly set back – a great model for a public
building, insinuating itself into the area while making no aesthetic
concessions to it. It's also a very strange design by E. A. Johnson,
a freestyle red-brick industrial Gothic with stepped, jagged buttresses. This too is long derelict, with its spiky silhouette made
even more wild by the overgrowth. Finally, just in between these
is an even stranger building, an exceptionally unusual structure

in any context – a synagogue, built in the 1870s, according to Pevsner (who cannot name the architect), the oldest purpose-built synagogue in Wales. It terminates the street abruptly, with high hills and trees just behind. There are three pointed towers, with a timber roof thrown arbitrarily between them, the symmetrical composition full with a compulsive upwards motion. Some of the windows are Gothic, some look like the windows of tenements. Long since disused by the town's Jewish residents, it had a spell as a health centre, but is empty and part boarded-up on the day we visit; a purple sign reading 'AUCTIONS' is slapped on it.

What complicates this picture of dereliction and decline is the spruceness of the houses themselves. It looks like Merthyr Tydfil's residents care for their area more than is common in the south-east of England. The terraces are spick, span and colourfully painted, rising up the slopes in parallel lines in a manner that makes me think inescapably of Brighton, absurd a comparison as that is. There's civic pride here, even if there isn't enough to keep all of the civic buildings open. At the town's centre is a gigantic Tesco, which from a hill looks exactly like the steelworks a supermarket inadequately replaces as generator of employment. A walk round here will unearth at least one recent building of some quality; a fish and chip shop, of all things, the Busy Bee Fish Bar & Café next to the optimistic Tourist Information Centre, is not half bad – a wood and metal pavilion with a big gabled roof that has escaped from an episode of *Grand Designs* and landed in one of the poorest areas in the UK. At the town's other exit is the recently closed streamline-moderne Hoover Factory, a dynamic design by Wallis Gilbert, architects of the more famous neo-Egyptian Hoover Building in Perivale. This one is a bit more restrained, a brick building with a dramatic curved corner, still heavily fenced-off, presumably to stop anyone from rummaging for scrap. Merthyr Tydfil also has a signposted 'Café Quarter', a square with a Chinese buffet and an iron bandstand, without a single person to be seen.

The next place we stop in is the village of Mountain Ash, in the Cynon Valley. Rows of precise, clipped council terraces lead towards one of the Valleys' several breath-stealing panoramic views, where the terraces, the hillsides and the variously derelict chapels and institutes come together in an accidental composition. The fulsome baroque town hall points out that it serves an 'urban district council', which answers the question as to whether the Valley villages are 'urban' or not, although Mountain Ash's population is just over 7000. That said, the place has bustling traffic at rush hour, as its inhabitants commute back from Cardiff and Newport. A lot of people here did, as IDS requested, get on their bikes, at least while they still could. A barn houses the local Citizens Advice Bureau. The landscape is magnificent, with forests of pine (apparently the result of post-war planning decisions) tightly enclosing what, for once, can aptly be called an urban village, a densely packed area that can be surveyed by the eye at once, that can be grasped as one entity. The hills make the place glorious as spectacle, and quite possibly, claustrophobic as a place to live.

Amazing Value

That certainly seems the case with Brynmawr, another series of terrace strips which once abutted the famous Brynmawr Rubber Factory, for a time Wales's most famous twentieth-century building. Its concrete vaults, designed by Architects Co-Partnership, were intended to house an industrial co-operative sponsored by the Attlee government. Privatised in less than a decade and eventually converted into a Semtex factory, it was demolished in 2001 in defiance of Grade II listing. From here, Ebbw Vale. After a few hours in this traumatic townscape, you could easily imagine terrorist cells emerging, avenging the damage done to the town and its people. The anti-tank measures and frisking at Cardiff's Senedd suddenly make sense. Follow the sign to the DHSS, and you can find some of the saddest sights in Britain. Worn, never-changed signs to the Civic Centre lead to a decent, if undemonstrative 1960s complex, its office blocks surrounded by the churned-up paving of a car park. A distressed leisure centre has what looks like a growth on it, the bright yellow and green tentacles of swimming pool flumes, with broken glass underneath. An angular underpass takes you to the rest of the town, and it has the most eloquent graffiti. 'AMAZING VALUE £5 – A WORKING CLASS HERO'. Then there's a small recreational ground, and the start of the terraces. The street lights are on. It's three o'clock in the afternoon, in July.

There's a lot to admire in Ebbw Vale; the incongruously tall, scraping spire of Christ Church, dwarfing the terraces, evidently intended to be a landmark for miles around; the compact centre,

with the unexpected joy of a bright red Festival of Britain interior in the Crossing Café; another sadly derelict, austere-baroque Workers' Institute; even the concrete car park at its centre, a fittingly muscular design reminiscent of Gateshead's demolished Trinity Car Park. This one was saved, but *improved* by being painted white and covered in metal wire. The public art here, in dismal contrast to Merthyr, is pro forma, a swooping metal clock surrounded by steel balls. It was commissioned the year after the steelworks closed; the site is still being cleared for impending 'regeneration', which may or may not have a positive effect. These things always feel like a sop, but the rest of the country owes Ebbw Vale and neighbouring Tredegar a favour, to say the least. On a hilltop between the two towns, commanding views of only partly re-landscaped industrial waste, surrounding works, terraces and hills that would be crammed with sightseers were they elsewhere, stands a memorial to NHS founder Aneurin Bevan. It's the most striking man-made object in the area, although it goes back to the very foundations of architecture: a stone circle, in the place where he used to speak to his constituents. It feels moving, mystical, an ancient monument to the belief in a viable future. We were there on the NHS's sixty-third birthday.

Tredegar has one of the Valleys' nearest things to a town plan – the centre revolves around an iron column with a clock on top. We pause in front of one shop, where a familiar face is superimposed onto a torch. This is the offices of 'Spirit of Bevan', a film co-operative, where we stop for a chat; the area's politics are proudly described to us as '*Old* Labour', but this place is seemingly more New Labour in form – a building for the cultural industry. Of course, that's a caricature: what the group does is catalogue the area's history and struggles, and offer a means of cultural production to those who usually don't have it, without the cant of Aspiration and Empowerment that comes with the idea of cultural replacing industrial production. The Spirit of Bevan people point out to us that the local miners' self-run health service was the NHS's original inspiration – Bevan merely intended to 'Tredegarize' the rest of the country. There's a little monument also to a more modernist social architecture in the form of Powell Alport and Partners' Tredegar Library, a striking, dynamic little piece of Brutalism, a riot of angles and geometries now accompanied by a mural depicting the town's radical heritage in naif style, a manner seldom used for the depiction of socialism and class struggle. It bears repeating that the idea of the National Health Service was born here, in this tiny and peculiar place. Not in Manchester, not in Birmingham, not in London. And as in the surrounding towns, all that the rest of the country can summon up to present in return is out-of-town retail parks and call centres. Right now, the gift is being thrown away regardless, in a de facto privatization. The groundwork for this was laid by the 'market reforms', foundation hospitals and 'market discipline' imposed under the last Labour government. There's a horrible trap at work here. Could the Valleys, with their evident and admirable refusal to forgive or forget, offer a way out of it?

In Search of the Silicon Valleys

In some of its policies, devolved Wales offers an insight into what Labour Britain might have been like if John Smith hadn't died. The reforms of Neil Kinnock, making Labour into a not-even-particularly Social Democratic, mildly left-of-centre Party,

were retained, while the full-on Blairite putsch for caring, sharing Thatcherism was quickly faced off in Wales. Rhodri Morgan's Welsh Labour Party have tried over the last decade to put 'Clear Red Water' between themselves and Millbank. There are no PFI hospitals in Wales, there are no prescription charges, and perhaps most startlingly, the Labour and Plaid Cymru-dominated Welsh Assembly has recently started to bring in curbs on the 'right' to buy council housing. To put that move into perspective, it occurs just when the Tory–Whig coalition in Westminster has been introducing limits to tenure, Housing Benefit caps and 'Right to Buy plus'. Here, a Labour vote is perhaps not entirely a grudging or tribal reflex. However, the South Wales landscape also makes it clear that this hypothetical John Smith-led new era would have taken substantially similar steps to attract investment – the courting of multinational capital to employ low-wage and low-security labour, the use of public–private partnerships for infrastructure (if not health), and an exurban, car-centred form of urban development. No doubt, the business parks on the edge of most Valleys towns would never have come into being without Labour authorities' lobbying and subsidy.

Blackwood is one town where the transition to the Silicon Valleys doesn't seem to have been entirely mythical, where a mining village has, arguably, become an exurb of Newport. It's one of the least peculiar-looking of these places; the immediate impression is of a West Midlands suburb that has been broken up and grafted onto series of lush hills; the houses that creep up them look a little larger and less harsh than in, say, Ebbw Vale or Mountain Ash, with gables and high pitched roofs. The high street, its shabby Victorian commerce interrupted by a big 1930s picture palace/Bingo Hall, has surely escaped from outer Birmingham. The Blackwood Miners Institute is not, at least, derelict. At the heart of the town is the most basic form of industrial replacement, a Big Shed retail development, housing a furniture store and a carvery. The finest piece of new architecture we see in the Valleys, by a long chalk, is here – Arup's Chartist Bridge, so named due to Blackwood's role in the Newport Rising of 1839. Opened in 2005, it's a sweeping cable-stayed bridge, simple and dramatic enough to shame all the Calatrava imitations. It's encouraging that this monument's function is to bring these scattered towns closer together. The main function, though, is as a conduit in the Sihowy Enterprise Way, an exurban drosscape leading to the Oakdale Business Park nearby, the part-constructed replacement for the Oakdale Colliery, largely courtesy of the European Union's Objective 1 fund. Next to this is a colossal socialist-realist sculpture of a Chartist, by Sebastian Boyesen. Constructed from steel mesh, it looks ghostly, the spectre of a power that has disappeared, for the moment.

In quite close proximity is the most futuristic structure in the area, a monument from the days when it seemed as if cybernetic industry might adopt a vivid and memorable physical form, rather than an immaterial anti-form, of giant white sheds producing tiny functional objects. In that, it's an interesting road not travelled. The building in question is the INMOS Microprocessor Factory in Duffryn, just on the outskirts of Newport, designed by Richard Rogers in 1980. It has none of the self-conscious warmth and 'humanism' of his Senedd in Cardiff, but marks an earlier, more fearless Rogers, who at that point surely expected that he'd spend much of the rest of his career designing factories, rather than luxury apartment complexes and prestigious cultural buildings. Like the Lloyds Building, it takes industrial process and makes it into melodrama, foregrounding cables, ducts, pipes, the sinews and tendons of production, and assembling them into a memorable image, as opposed to just putting everything into a big box. And, unlike many a celebrated architect-designed industrial building, it still does what it was built for – the production of microprocessors, currently for the delightfully-named International Rectifier.

From here we head into Newport itself, the aforementioned friend's home town, to have a brief look round before heading back to England. Newport's cohesive, impressive face from the train is not entirely borne out on the ground, with some exceptionally heavy interventions by 1970s road engineers taking much of the pleasure out of the Usk riverscape; but it's hard to castigate a place for being car-centred when riding in a car. We're going to have a look at Newport Docks, especially at its Transporter Bridge. The way there takes us past several clearly just-finished boom-era developments, surely likely to sit empty for some time. 'NEWHAUS – Contemporary Riverside Apartments'. Deutschlish is one way of avoiding the imperative to bilingual signs. The rain now becomes a Biblical torrent which makes the bridge look doubly ethereal, a far more spindly and delicate structure than that at Middlesbrough. This is the sort of tradition that Rogers must have thought he was working in at INMOS – the monumental display of industry and technology, proud and unashamed, the focus for the entire landscape. Opposite, in amongst the long, low sheds and battered brick factories, is a large Victorian hotel, with a bulbous, baroque clock tower. Someone must have wanted to stay here.

Chapter Fourteen

Edinburgh: Capital (It Fails Us Now)

The Scottish Difference

The question keeps coming back when thinking about the possible future of the United Kingdom. What if Scotland could be different? Fifteen years after devolution, a year after the Scottish National Party's landslide victory in the elections to the Scottish Parliament, and a year (if Cameron has his way) or two years (if Salmond has his) before a referendum on Independence, Scotland might be just about to flee the sinking ship. In this, the SNP have proven to be genuinely skilled politicians in a world of blagging PR wonks. Their left face is more convincing and concrete than Labour's, involving real policies such as getting rid of prescription charges and refusing to bring in tuition fees (except for English and Welsh students, of course), an effective opposition to PFI hospitals and health care 'reform', and a mild anti-imperialism that would also entail withdrawal of Trident. Their right face, meanwhile, is enough to gain even the support of Murdoch: a craven attitude towards finance capital, low-taxation policies, a (now-lapsed) enthusiasm for erstwhile neoliberal 'tigers' such as Ireland and Iceland, and a courting of hard-right privateers like Stagecoach boss Brian Souter. In that, they're not so much Tartan Tories as Tartan Lib Dems. Given that the Whig 'left' has evaporated in obsequious gratitude to a skewed coalition with the Tories, there is reason to be suspicious. The SNP is an opportunist Party, all things to all people, but one which has shifted Scottish politics way to the left of England's.

That might just presage the shape of the future Scottish Free State.

A trip to Edinburgh, then, should hopefully present something quite different, something more optimistic, than can be found south of the border. Scotland has a far more convincing tradition of urbanism than England. Its cities are northern European, not quasi-American. The four-storey tenements of Scottish cities are, when you strip all the history and the myth from them, simply the most imposing, convincing and cohesive form of mass architecture anywhere in the UK, both in their working- and middle-class versions; all the demands in the New Labour Urban Renaissance policy documents basically amounted to asking for the rest of Britain to be more like the West Ends of Edinburgh and Glasgow. The town plans of Glasgow, Aberdeen and of course Edinburgh are masterful creations, of a sort rare in England outside of tourist reservations like Bath (or Newcastle, which urbanistically speaking is a Scottish Exclave). This superiority is hardly limited to electoral politics or eighteenth- and nineteenth-century urbanism. For the last thirty years Scotland has had more skilled and original modernist novelists, less heritage-kitschy and exploitative film-makers, a less coked-up and obnoxious music scene, than England. It has a Conservative Party so tiny and marginalized that many of its high-ups are considering changing the Party's name in order to 'detoxify the brand'. It also has some of the poorest areas in Europe, some of the most luxuriantly corrupt, now-bailed-out banks, and a gap between rich and poor that rivals England's. There's not quite clear red water between the two, but definitely a pinkish sludge.

In contemporary architecture too, perhaps, Scotland might prove to have achieved something different. A tradition of living in flats and planning cities, a historic embrace of the sublime and powerful rather than the picturesque and pretty-pretty, are factors that ought to make a difference. Architects such as Malcolm Fraser, Elder & Cannon, Benson & Forsyth, Gareth Hoskins, the recently defunct gm&ad, or English expat Richard Murphy, all consider themselves proper urbanists and serious civic designers, rather than iconists or tinkerers. Housing Associations, until recently, still built a lot more up here than south of the border. So can this country, which never bought into Thatcherism, offer a potential way out?

For those of us, like the present writer, who have never been to Edinburgh before, Waverley Station offers two very different introductions. First, you arrive in the most chaotically planned railway station, much of it under scaffolding, a multilevel maze; the first thing you see when leaving the King's Cross train is a cluster of police vans. Walk round this station a little bit and you find a grand, top-lit neoclassical entrance hall that was clearly once very elegant. At the centre of it is a little pod housing a branch of Costa Coffee. Anti-pigeon netting hovers above it like cobwebs, and no less than twelve CCTV cameras flank the edges, in case you were planning to loot a latte. Scottish Home Rule might well be making this overwhelmingly left-wing country a more humane place than its southern neighbour, but this station is a sight which could only be found in Great Britain. Heavy security, blaring commerce, mistreated imperial grandeur, confusing non-planning, all are present and correct.

Find your way out of the station, though, and you see something else, and the suffocating Festival crowds become irrelevant. A Victorian-futurist bridge soars high overhead, and its plunge bisects two tall towers, masonry on steel frames – baroque in theory, Gothic in practice. It's a scene as excitingly metropolitan as anything you'll find in Scotland's de facto rather than de jure capital in Glasgow, and it instantly replaces the initial feeling of irritation and dread with one of expectation and anticipation. Look to one side of this amazing *mise-en-scène* and you find a brutally craggy Acropolis; look to the other side and there's a planned neoclassical city of great urbanity. Familiarity with Edinburgh might well breed contempt, but my first reaction was speechless awe. And awe especially at how this unusual and dramatic form of urbanism can have become so popular, with the teeming crowds all around. Take Edinburgh and make it into a list of things people like in cities, and you'll find it highly counter-intuitive. What people like, apparently, is highly coherent and even authoritarian town planning, steep and melodramatic topography, very tall buildings, the total dominance of flats, with hardly any single-family houses to be seen – and sombre, dark colour everywhere, with only tiny hints of the bright, the rustic or the twee. It doesn't even feel like a ceremonial capital, with the real action in Glasgow. In other places that it might be compared to – Bath, or Durham – were tourism to be taken away the whole thing might disappear, whereas in Edinburgh it feels as if the city could get along very nicely without all this unseemly bustle, thank you very much.

The Only Fun in Town

I received a quick lesson in Edinburgh topography by travelling west through the Georgian gridiron of the New Town, watching it gradually devolve into tenements that could be easily relocated to Glasgow, then past a large (and here, especially incongruously crap) 2000s school, eventually ending up at Fettes College, a Victorian Gothic design by David Bryce. It is absolutely enormous, Gothic taken literally, to the point of horror. It's housing a series of events on public art, so the entrance towers have in front of them giant cubic cats, with interactive exhibits inside. Slightly less prominent are 1960s low-rise additions, in expensively finished metal and stone. Fettes College is Tony Blair's alma mater. Like the travails of RBS, it's a reminder that the British ruling class is not at all exclusive to England. As a piece of architecture, resistance to it is futile. The College has a darkling presence on the skyline in this end of Edinburgh, its blackened, gory concoction of ever-more spindly and sharp towers protruding over an area of privilege as marked as anything in Mayfair.

Yet it is also an area of flats, and flats built as flats. The axis leading away from it is lined by inter-war tenements, showing the basic components of Scottish mass housing – the stone, the dignified austerity, the high windows, the scraggy backsides that you aren't supposed to look at – starting to accommodate a few cosmetic features from the modern movement, such as moderne typography, glazed stairwells and the elimination of previous tenements' already minimal ornament. At this point, one wonders what might have happened if this minor reform had been taken as a model for post-war urban mass housing in Scotland; if there had been a gradual repair and expansion of its working-class cities, rather than a botched revolution. This is at least the thought that stays with you until visiting Leith, when you find far less attractive working-class inter-war tenements. Such a reformist approach could easily have been as grim as the towers and low-rises that eventually got built. That said, the pattern was actually being broken around here even then – after those neat '30s tenements, you encounter a Mansion Block that completely breaks with the compact streetline and openness, creating instead a large, insular complex, albeit one still detailed with the same square bay windows. Up the hill a bit, past someone's baronial fantasy of a stand-alone tenement, and you reach the Western edges of the New Town, in the form of the Moray Estate. Call me obvious, but it's glorious, unforgettable. First there's a bridge over a canyon, from which you can see the backs of the tenements rising out of the rock like a craggy *Metropolis*, or look out towards Leith's grain silos and the Firth of Forth; after that, you come to Randolph Cliff, and a half-crescent sweeps you into an environment of awesome urbanity; but its urge to create monumental order is constantly subverted by an unwilling topography that dips out of it, thrusts into it, leaving its unseemly posterior visible to the walker. The 'Athenian' aspiration is not at all mock-Mediterranean – the blackened sandstone is utterly northern. A junction pivots on American-styled inter-war offices and a red sandstone bank, both fugitives from Glasgow, and you're at Princes Street.

Princes Street is a one-sided, monumental avenue, punctuated by the sound of bagpipes and with all the Scottish Tat shops that you never find in Glasgow. Architecturally, it's not so much the built-up side that you notice, as the enfilade of towers running along the gardens and the railway embankment below; the freakish, untutored, charred Gothic of the Scott Monument, the Victorian baroque tower of the North British Hotel, leading eventually to the National Monument's instant ruin, and in the distance further follies dedicated to Nelson and Burns. All of them are in different styles, all of them are more than slightly absurd, and all of them seem strangely coherent, designed to be viewed together. Turn towards the Old Town and you find the temporary architecture of the Festival; corporate-branded pink inflatables, a geodesic dome, the techniques of 1960s utopianism

used, as intended, in the service of disposability and leisure, although not, as also intended, encompassing the entire city. Another form of 1960s architecture can be seen on Princes Street itself, in the results of the 'Princes Street Panel'. This was a plan to restore the Georgian order to a street made eclectic and kitsch by the Victorians, although Georgian in spirit rather than letter – masonry façades on concrete and steel frames, with unused first-floor promenades across them. They're all very professional and fairly elegant, though the failure to encompass the whole street rather defeats the object – but the idea is quite an interesting misunderstanding of what seems (to me, at least) the interesting thing about Edinburgh – the way that its attempts to create order are constantly assaulted by topography and fashion.

That's not to say that every attempt to upend Georgian rationalism here is worthwhile. The complex of accretions known as 'St James Shopping' is a structure whose ability to have received planning permission even in the 1960s is truly extraordinary; unlike the Princes Street Panel's conscientious attempt to produce a twentieth-century Edinburgh, this is a piece of pure, principle-free speculation with few redeeming features – and which, to make it worse, appears unstoppable, growing and morphing yet never acquiring a personality. You first see the earliest part of the St James Centre in the form of a Thistle Hotel, straggling insultingly in front of the axial vista of Archibald Elliott's Waterloo Place. Its recent redevelopment compounds the injury, labouring under the twin misapprehensions that it can all be made better via wonky, 'friendly' shapes (iconic!) and stone-cladding (contextual!). In fact, the general fearless barbarity of the original 1960s shopping centre does provide one impressive view, where it appears as a concrete castle, rising to a central keep – but this aspect turns its face to alleyways and a bus station, rather than the boozy public thoroughfare of Leith Street. If you walk around those alleyways, the ruthless commercial interventions start to take on a more positive dystopian quality. Waterloo Place is carried over Calton Road by the neoclassical Regent Bridge, and from around here you can see gigantic, ancient-looking tenements traversed by bulbous, trussed Blairite walkways. There's a great twenty-first-century metropolitan redevelopment of Edinburgh in here somewhere, hidden by cowardice and thuggery.

First, a walk round the back-end of the Eastern New Town, or rather the Calton, a hilltop development where the topography seems to have been worked with rather than against. The dark, austere Royal Terrace and its continuations do manage to curve with the contours of the hill, and present an especially striking vision of affluence – houses so expensive that most of them are hotels or diplomatic premises, well protected against the hoi polloi. If you follow the sweep around here, you get to St Andrew's House, a 1930s government building designed by modernizing classicist Thomas Tait, responsible for many fine buildings in Glasgow, London and elsewhere, as well as the first modernist estate in the UK (that one's in Braintree). Due to its architectural authoritarianism and it being merely the branch for a Scottish Office based in London, this building is occasionally considered by Scottish Nationalists to be the headquarters of an occupying power. Be that as it may politically, architecturally the structure presents two very different faces. To the street, it is an ordered essay in art deco, with echoes (in the cubic lamp standards and gates) of constructivism and (in much else) the reduced classicism of the Italian Novecento. To the cliffs of the Old Town, it's something far more exciting – a building which, like the earlier 'Athenian' Edinburgh, takes an international style and makes it look entirely indigenous, intrinsic to the landscape, its heavy stone volumes stepping down the crags. It makes no 'references', but feels organic to the landscape in a corporeal, non-rhetorical way. It's a good place to disembark for the Old Town, in order to find the more recent expression of Scottish self-government.

The Radical Legacies of Conservative Surgery

The most picturesque, if also the most crowded approach to the Old Town is along the North Bridge, where its essential inauthenticity is at its most aesthetically invigorating. The two entrance towers are extraordinary, ten-storey Victorian high-rises. They're not steel-framed, structure-expressing near-skyscrapers of the sort you find often in Glasgow, but the better-built extension of the mammoth tenements indigenous to the Old Town – structures which can present four storeys to the polite end of the street and ten to the back end, an extreme form of the 'upstairs/ downstairs' division in English domestic architecture. One of them is the original offices of *The Scotsman*, the other a hotel – neither particularly medieval typologies. Walk from here through an arcade, and you're in the 'original' Old Town, an elaborate, well-kept stage set full of secrets and subterfuge, well worth an extensive exploration if you can bear being importuned every five seconds by awful performers and flyers for stand-up comedians. The Festival's temporary architecture is rather more direct here – a big sponsorship banner from Virgin Money, with the Huxleyesque legend 'Because everybody joins in, everybody's better off'.

Edinburgh Old Town, facing as it does the *tabula rasa* of the New, is the font of a planning tradition that is the opposing force to all *grands projets*. That's not the tradition of the ad hoc medieval city itself, but the still-extant late-nineteenth-century rehabilitation of it, alternately for intellectuals and for its once-extensive working-class population. This is the legacy of Patrick Geddes, the late-nineteenth/early-twentieth-century planner who recommended 'conservative surgery' to repair slum districts

– which the tall, late medieval or Renaissance tenements of the Old Town certainly were when he started writing. The things about Edinburgh that are charming rather than merely impressive often stem from this. Ramsay Garden, the 'Renaissance' towers just by the castle, jutting out towards the ridge, visible from Princes Street, is one of Geddes' interventions, and was initially let to students in order to get the middle classes back into the Old Town, to remake the famously foul 'auld Reekie' into something where medieval creepiness was evoked as an aesthetic and a memory, rather than a pungent reality. This was, in its way, very original indeed. Geddes evidently looked at architecture and planning that was indelibly associated with slums, a teeming and restless proletariat, squalor and disease, and saw in it a problem that could be entirely separated from its buildings, resolved without clearance or reconstruction, with the structures capable of being enjoyed for their architectonic qualities, with their associations very much secondary. It's not a model that was fully accepted elsewhere until the 1970s, but here in the Old Town it has evidently had a century or so to do its work. In making the students of Edinburgh University central to this 'rehabilitation', Geddes could be regarded as an exceptionally early prophet of what we now know as 'gentrification'. Yet, at least at first, the Old Town's workers were as much a subject of this project as students. Round the other side of the Castle are very early (1900) council flats by the City Improvement Trust at Portsburgh Square, very much under Geddes's influence – neo-Scots architecture with iron deck-access walkways. Around the freakish, fairytale Grassmarket there are more of these, much later – 1970s and 80s Housing Association versions, usually without the stonework, a little thin and contrived, but nonetheless providing cheap rents in an area that many rich Scots-Americans would give their fortunes to lodge within.

When you descend through Cowgate, it's much easier to imagine the slum this once was – the bridges that were thrown across here to make it easier for those upstairs to get around still cast the area into gloom, and the effect still has traces of the H. G. Wells/*Metropolis*-like division of Victorian Edinburgh into Eloi and Morlocks. There's a large Housing Association

scheme by Richard Murphy worth a glance, but more interesting is the plaque opposite, dedicated to the Marxist revolutionary
James Connolly, who was born here, before gaining fame as an
agitator in America and martyrdom in Ireland. Later, reading
C. Desmond Greaves's biography of Connolly, I found the claim
that Edinburgh was initially more of a socialist stronghold than
the future Red Clydeside, but that slum clearance and rehousing in the Old Town had dispersed and tamed its insurgent
proletariat. In that sense at least, conservative surgery really was
Conservative, in the sense of being a safeguard against revolution. The circle has turned so sharply towards laissez-faire since
then that it once again seems sharply radical. The very notion
of providing working-class housing in a place like this! For a
London equivalent to the abundant public housing on and around
the Royal Mile, imagine council flats on Whitehall.

Canongate, the bottom end of the Royal Mile, shows this
incongruity to its full extent. Here, tiny council estates, designed
by Basil Spence in an unpretentious grey and brown Scottish
Brutalist-Vernacular, or by Robert Hurd in an arcaded neoclassicism evocative of reconstructed post-war Central Europe,
are as dignified and decorous as their repaired and renovated
pre-modern forbears. The estate at the very foot of the hill is

Dumbiedykes, a standard, well-proportioned post-war council estate without any major nods towards its exalted setting, looking entirely unassuming in front of the outrageous topography of Arthur's Seat. That's something to celebrate, needless to say. If you follow the alleyways and stairwells off Spence's estate, you can find a Housing Association scheme, Morgan Court, designed in 1998 by Ungless & Latimer. The flats are relatively brightly coloured in red, white, blue, as had been some of the Geddes-inspired interventions a century ago, although the effect is a little closer to the palette of contemporary regen. There's another Housing Association estate nearby by Richard Murphy, of quasi-modernist 'tower house' tenements, which likewise falls somewhere in between orthodoxy and originality. Both are asymmetrical and ingeniously planned for their cramped sites, and in both, the tight organization and the surprising public spaces work very well together. This is, then, a living tradition, and sets the mind wandering. What if Bow or the Gorbals were treated like this in the 1960s? Repaired not by traditionalists, but alternately patched-up, sensitively infilled, and set in contrast with similarly scaled but aesthetically disjointed new developments, all managing to retain the atmosphere and feel of a teeming, friendly area while upgrading its amenities, sanitation, facilities and suchlike? Here, it seems to work, although the tourists must get on the nerves of the council tenants.

Holyrood Freaks

This seeming success makes it all the more disappointing that the most recent additions to the Old Town at Holyrood are so grindingly identikit, so quintessentially British, that they bring the place immediately crashing back down to earth. They include bank and newspaper offices, luxury flats, and a hotel, all of a very poor architectural quality, all on an incredibly prominent site. The largest are the blocks of the Park complex, planned by architects Campbell & Arnott (who went bust in 2010). Then there's the Macdonald Hotel, a vaguely postmodernist gabled block of similarly tacky materials. Both are roughly the right scale for the place, but in cheap and nasty materials – rendered concrete, already stained and streaky, but with none of the tactile surfaces that can be found in the council housing nearby. There are classic 2000s bolted-on balconies, and there is slatted wood. Worse still are the offices, such as the curving, stone-faced wobbly-roofed buildings for *The Scotsman* and Citigroup by Comprehensive Design Architects, which don't even have the metropolitan proportions of the hotels and flats – just speculative office blocks that could be found absolutely anywhere in the UK, irrespective of the thin ashlar facing. The whole set-up closely resembles the shopping-mall vernacular additions to the St James Centre – and so it should, being by the same architects. Then there's The Tun, by Alan Murray, a verdigris block whose leaning form is inescapably in the 'iconic' mode. We're just opposite Arthur's Seat, and the Scottish Parliament. How did a site so important end up being botched like this? Small-scale gems like Malcolm Fraser's Poetry Library in Canongate itself, or Richard Murphy's very convincing Fruitmarket Gallery further into the centre, or other minor interventions to be found all over the city prove that Edinburgh has architects fit for the task. There's evidently a rule that Edinburgh gives its large projects to large firms and small projects to small firms. Unfortunately, the large firms tend to be nondescript corporate hacks. In the process, Edinburgh seems to be replicating the race to the bottom found in other British cities, though its wealth, importance and civic culture, suggest it should be in a better position than most to avoid it.

They do still work within Geddes's limits in the Old Town – the new Scottish spec architecture has a much larger enclave, which we'll get to later. But on brief acquaintance, there are two large-scale structures in Edinburgh after Geddes that abandon conservative surgery and instead go for the drastic and risky operation, one high-end, one low. The latter, the St James Centre, we've already discussed; the other is the Scottish Parliament, designed by the late Enric Miralles and Benedetta Tagliabue. This is a building that fully deserves to be taken seriously, however much bullshit and cant may have been expended on it as a topic. Unlike most monuments to Regeneration, which are generally one-liners that can be appraised at a glance, shape-making of little more complexity than the average corporate logo, this is a

building of fragments, passageways and alleys – an architectural montage with geological pretensions. Spreading into pieces at the foot of the hill, it defies glib analysis – it must be one of the only major projects of the last two decades to have managed to avoid acquiring a jolly nickname. It's flattered further by being placed next to a simple mini-Millennium Dome by Michael Hopkins, 'Dynamic Earth' – not awful in itself, but tellingly different; English technocratic architecture, unwilling or unable to make the site's appropriate statements about regionalism, independence and nationality.

The rationale behind choosing the experimental Catalan architects was a shared experience of devolution, with Edinburgh's claim to being the Barcelona of the North more geopolitically convincing than Manchester's. It's a neat gesture. If you're walking to the Parliament from the Royal Mile, your first sight of it is an angular volume, itself held up on a concrete crag, breaking off from the streetline. Set into it are various quotes in English, Scots and Scots Gaelic expressing valediction in escaping from 'Lunnon' along with various other pearls of wisdom, some annoying, some very funny, most appropriate. Then, opposite Holyrood Park, the entire ensemble stretches itself out in front of a magnificently public park, framing the view of Arthur's Seat. The architecture is obsessively busy. A partial inspiration seems to be the Glaswegian Charles Rennie Mackintosh, the architect of world-changing genius that Edinburgh never managed to produce. Like Mackintosh's, Miralles and Tagliabue's architecture is the kind that provokes questions about *what the architect is trying to tell us here*; the façade positively begs for such speculation. Why those cow-like black shapes bolted elliptically onto the windows? Why the random wood outcrops bolted alongside? Why is the public entrance so low and cave-like? Some of these puzzles are obviously deliberate, but it's not a particularly interesting game to play. More intriguing is to chart on foot something much clearer from the mountain – the building's exploded form, assembled into several discrete parts, connected by raw concrete walkways. You can only get little glimpses of it as a pedestrian wandering around, or as pedestrian not on a guided tour, but it's here at the back, where the occasionally too whimsical play of forms and oblique signs meets a heavy, physical tectonic mass, that the building really thrills.

Aside from the park that flows out towards Arthur's Seat, the most striking strictly *urban* aspect of the Scottish Parliament is how Miralles and Tagliabue, or their executive architects RMJM, specifically tried to design the ubiquitous security features of a contemporary government building. Rather than leaving it to the council, the architects helpfully provided bristly organic high fences and sensually curved concrete blast walls. This takes on an extra resonance when you find that some of the estates in Canongate have been slated for demolition; evidently the Scottish Parliament isn't entirely comfortable with even a tamed, well-housed working-class population so close by. No Scottish cities rioted in the month when we were wandering round Edinburgh, unlike practically every large English city except Sheffield, a cause for some self-congratulation north of the border; but that doesn't mean they're not hedging their bets.

Bad Banks and Their Bad Buildings

On the second of the two summertime visits to Edinburgh, we were staying in a tenement in Morningside, an affluent suburb to the south of the city centre. A route from there into town was a vivid journey through this mini-Metropolis, and one that also entailed initial excitement and final disappointment. Morningside itself is a marvellous place, a sleepy series of monumental tenement-lined streets containing a cornucopia of charity shops, a testament to the civic virtues of the Edinburgh bourgeois. The pleasure here, architecturally, is mostly in watching the tenements stride out towards another close, elemental, mountainous landscape in the south (with Arthur's Seat visible just to the east), but there's some interest to be found in the smaller buildings. There's the moderne Dominion cinema, some aggressive, demonstrative churches, and a pub, The Merlin, that presents a faceted glass front to the street, designed by Chris Stewart in 2002. That a new pub would be of such quality is a sure sign of affluence, and of the very active civic society and architectural watchdog groups that tend to come with it. The closer you get to the centre, the larger and more grandiose the tenements become, the more their architects (or, more realistically, their builders) seem to be playing with the looming, intimidating qualities of the form; stretching the bay windows upwards with the high ceilings, adding bloody great conical turrets onto them, as if in megacity competition with the industrial metropolis on the west coast.

When this meets the Old Town, various modern interventions move into this darkling ashlar streetscape. The earliest is the 1930s St Cuthbert's Co-Operative Building in Bread Street, a rare architectural example of Edinburgh pioneering rather than critically assimilating. Set into a row of Victorian stone tenements, it's a sheer glass curtain wall, recently adapted reasonably faithfully (architecturally rather than ethically) into a Conference Centre. Its advanced glass structure was unusual for the UK at the time (if not for Germany, Holland or Czechoslovakia), but the curio value lies in representing a very early essay in the notion that a neutral glass addition to a historic building structure is the way to show effective respect, without the pieties of staying 'in keeping'.

That has since become the orthodox way of building extensions to art galleries and such, to the regular spleen of *Private Eye*'s architectural correspondent 'Piloti'. This is a very fine early example of the form, sitting in the middle of the street as if bridging it. Or maybe it just seems elegant in comparison with the architectures that would follow it.

It's at this point, in Tollcross, that the architecture of Scottish finance capitalism can be fully appreciated, if that's the right word – a centre of various banks and insurers more dense than any to be found outside of London. If there's a comparison to be made, it's less to the new architecture of the English capital and more to Leeds. The Yorkshire city's masonry-mixed-with-high-tech style is the nearest equivalent in architectural manner, but not quite in scale – while Leeds banks wilfully go up to twenty storeys plus, you can't quite get away with that in Edinburgh, as the recent furore over a proposed Richard Murphy tower by Haymarket Station made very clear. The reduced height, of course, always means a translation into greater bulk, into spreading, corpulent width. There's a common language here, to the point where it looks like there were strict design guidelines. To the street, a line of ashlar cladding, studded with irregular fenestration; to the corners and intersections, large expanses of glass, preferably either curved or pointed for maximum 'iconic' effect, just in case anyone thought the aesthetic was a little staid. The men in dark suits stride purposefully from one to the other.

As to what we're looking at here – there's the Princes Exchange, designed in 2001 by PJMP architects, probably the most obnoxious of these structures. It takes up an entire block, on a roughly triangular plan. The style derives at several removes from Richard Rogers and Norman Foster, with glass stair towers, shiny metallic cladding and mock-industrial gob-ons, which has now gone worn and seedy. The front façade, with its glazed outlook tower, houses Lloyds, the back gets the Bank of Scotland, as if to presage some future bankruptcy-induced merger. A little better is the slightly earlier Scottish Widows HQ by BDP, which is a straight crib from Michael Hopkins's designs for the Inland Revenue in Nottingham – a not-too-modernized image of bureaucracy, where the integration between stone and glass has been achieved with relative skill, ashlar columns placed between fairly elegant oriel windows. A similar style is followed by Terry Farrell, the MI6 architect who was until recently official 'design adviser' to the Scottish capital, in the Edinburgh International Conference Centre. This large stone rotunda is fearsomely unlovely and overbearing, made even more vast by a recent BDP extension. As the expression of basically corrupt institutions with ancient roots who have recently become notorious for making reckless use of new computational methods with disastrous results, it's architecturally as clear and apt as could be. As a piece of townscape, it's painful in its clumsy alternation between aggression and blandness. The delicate surgical interventions, fantasies and Brutalist fancies in the Old Town seem a long way away.

The Surgeon Falters

Given that the riots in England and Wales occurred the month I visited Scotland, I was regularly reminded by proud Scots of the absence of civil unrest in the northerly part of the island. One of the many possible explanations for this centres on the different structure of Scottish cities. Although Glasgow and Edinburgh do have 'mixed' districts – the Old Town proves to be a surprising example – their 'European' nature extends to localizing extreme poverty in distant settlements, cut off from public transport, employment and civic life – Easterhouse or Drumchapel in Glasgow, Muirhouse or Niddrie in Edinburgh. Given its Irvine Welsh–mediated reputation, I had assumed Leith to be one of these peripheral, class-segregated places, a Forthside *banlieue*. The way that people I spoke to in Edinburgh talked as if Leith was not part of the city ('Oh, we didn't really have an industrial working class here. Except for Leith') seemed to support the idea. I was to be very surprised. Leith is a place as much marked by the very poor living next to the very comfortable as can be found in the East End of London. It's a town with a great and sombre power all of its own, and a place which displays a contrast between Geddes-issue repair and rehabilitation, and *tabula rasa* sweep, as stark as in Edinburgh itself.

Depending on the bus you take into Leith, you can pass

along impressive and harsh sandstone tenements in a straight line to the sea, or you can take a perhaps more instructive route round the houses. That bus route takes you past the Hibernian stadium, and the large and completely nondescript, car-centred Meadowbank retail park, housing Bingo, M&S, TK Maxx and KFC. The latter is most strange to find so very close to central Edinburgh, as opposed to in a much smaller, poorer town, or more usually, on such a town's outskirts. Doesn't this place have any self-respect? A clue as to why this was permitted is offered when the bus takes you through some typical Leith housing. The bland interwar tenements are the concomitant to the elegant 1930s efforts glimpsed earlier near Fettes College. The tenement tradition continued, by all means, with the same relation to the street, the same scale, the same density, the same closeness to amenities and work, all the things that led to their reappraisal in the wake of Scotland's modernist period – but in execution they were immeasurably poorer, pebble-dashed and marked on the façade by big utilitarian drainpipes. Oddly, class difference is actually less palpable in the contrast between Victorian tenements in Leith and in Morningside, although that wouldn't have been true of the interior organization, to put it delicately. The other, more optimistic straight route to the sea, shows what at first looks like a completely coherent working-class extension of Edinburgh. Then you start noticing the sheer amount of new buildings, on what would once have been gap sites and wastelands, and realize that a major work of conservative surgery has taken place here. Leith has been patched up and resuscitated, with infill blocks for private landlords, Housing Associations or both, restoring what must have been long-disrupted streetlines.

So you can follow that main approach to the sea and turn into the grand, imposing entry point to the docks, and find something pretty much as impressive as anything else here. The classical showpieces – the Custom House, the Exchange – are superb, austere and so soot-blackened that they assume a very different face to the sandblasted Edinburgh streetscape. The commercial and residential buildings too are darker, rougher, somewhere between port and fishing village. The dominant colour is black. Given how smooth this approach to Leith is, could it have been that pre-crash Leith was an Urban Renaissance success story? However sensible Geddes-style incremental planning might be for these sorts of dense, highly developed areas, they rest on a certain degree of architectural skill that, for some unfathomable reason, has been absent in recent additions, so there can be a fair bit of quibbling about the quality of the surgery. The patient may have been saved, but the stitching can look quite untutored. The prettiest part of central Leith, the Shore, is a great example of this, as the infill, while perfectly scaled to the surroundings, is too often on the wrong side of twee, or worse, cheap. What makes Leith especially interesting is that here, you can watch the urban planning interventions under the contrasting influences of Patrick Geddes and Le Corbusier fighting it out in exceptionally close proximity.

Leith was subject to dramatic slum clearances, and the largest-scale result of this, the architectural event of Leith in many ways, is Cables Wynd House, designed in the mid-1960s by Alison Hutchinson and Partners – an immense concrete Unité d'Habitation that sweeps sinuously past dense alleys and side-streets. It's a fine, even heroic work of architecture on a magnificent scale, but perhaps less impressive as urbanism, with the car parking block of these 'Banana Flats' a barrier between itself and the rest of the city. What is plainer, however, is that this place actually manages to solve the question of keeping the non-affluent in the centre better than the small-scale Geddesian interventions. Housing Association developments tend to provide for a mix of public tenancies subsidized by private renting/buying – so, in short, the amount of people they can take off the council waiting list is fairly minimal. The Banana Block is sweeping in its politics as much as in its form, scooping the area up and rehousing it in something grandiose and highly public, a monumental form which necessarily dominates everything around it – a focus, a place which shows itself off. If there is a fight here between the two approaches, the strength of this block means we'd have to call it a draw.

At the heart of the new Leith is a less informal piece of town planning: the Scottish Office, now the Scottish Government, designed in the mid-90s by RMJM. The gating here isn't playing the coy games that EMBT used at Holyrood, but is a perimeter fence that you wouldn't want to fuck with, a paranoid panorama of business-park misery. It's central to the transformation of the derelict port via the pepper-potting of office blocks, luxury flats and bistros, all of which sit next to stark poverty – in Leith, as in London, you really can walk in seconds from the glass-strewn forecourts of semi-derelict estates to Michelin-starred restaurants. It's lively, and the pubs are excellent, but it's all a bit unnerving. One stretch of high-end restaurants is just opposite the security gates for the Government offices, a straight line. They're part of a warehouse conversion.

Speculation, Reindustrialization, Dereliction

What makes the above somewhat unfair is that there is a place in Leith where large-scale, *tabula rasa* development has been attempted, and it is not good. Leith Dock is an unbelievable mess, an enormous and hellish swathe of vacuous, lowest-common-denominator development that would shame a southern English town, let alone the Scottish capital. It is a complete disaster, whose lineaments are so vast as to be hard to describe, whether

in architectural or political terms. It's no use blaming it on the direct context. Leith itself, especially after its recent patching-up, can nearly hold its own with the city centre in its muscular, robust neoclassicism; even the immediate industrial context can be architecturally dramatic and worthwhile – the entirety of Leith Docks is overlooked by a massive, Americanist Concrete Atlantis of a grain silo, far more of an icon than anything built facing it. And the most obvious point: this is a short bus ride from an extremely rich city centre, a capital both administrative, at the Parliament (which, as noted, even has a branch here), and financial, with all the monstrous offices on Tollcross. That city has been responsible for two of the most impressive acts of town planning in European history, the neophile sweep of James Craig's original New Town and the more recent, carefully-tended montage of the Old Town. It has, again as you can verify in the Old Town, several very skilled and imaginative contemporary architects. The place also has an original and deeply local planning and architectural tradition, a degree of political independence, and a wise distrust of public–private partnerships. Literally everything was on their side here, so how did they manage to create something so awful?

It's best, for contrast, to head off towards the Leith Docks redevelopment from the Exchange and Custom House. The tenements and infill stop abruptly at one point, where you can see the Mint Casino as your entrance to the new. It's clad in pinkish stone, with a green glass entrance portal, the rest of the façade marked only by tiny square windows. There are better buildings in retail parks in Charlton. The riverside walk, Ocean Way, is scrubby and fenced-off, with weeds growing where the public promenade should be. There are several different versions of the basic flat form, but they're all similarly shoddy. Eight storeys is the norm, usually with some staggering of skylines so that we don't spot how monolithic it all is, all dressed up in the most basic and clumsy way, with Trespa hoods over the windows, dozens of gobbed-on metal balconies, fences and random protrusions, and the ubiquitous wonky roof is resorted to on every possible occasion. I'm not exaggerating here – this is actively on the level of the worst student housing in Leicester, the most egregious new yuppiedromes in Birmingham, the naffest exurban abortions in

Dartford. It puts certain things in perspective, too – other mer-etricious yuppie colonies from the Olympic Village to Glasgow Harbour suddenly look by comparison like, well, Edinburgh New Town. The centrepiece of the whole thing is an enclosed shopping mall, known as Ocean Terminal, a (Conran-designed!) mall exactly like any other mall; next to it in the wasteland is Ocean Point, a nondescript office block that, for once, is not even pretending to be friendly. That's by Sir Terry Farrell, but much of this ensemble is by a firm called Gilbert Associates, about whom I could discover nothing more than that they have their offices on Grassmarket. One of the blocks on Ocean Drive has an all-but illegible inscription, which when you look up close reveals itself to be the imprint of an erased RBS logo.

So who is to blame? The site is owned and run by Forth Ports, the privatized successors of the nationalized dock company, who are doubtless lacking in expertise for the development of new urban districts. The original plans by RMJM were harshly and rightly criticized, and then replaced with new guidelines by Winchester neoclassicist Robert Adam. In this chaos, neoclassicism's staid certainties should be relatively welcome, but the succession of plans doesn't change the fact that the actual execution is always in the hands of whichever developers each slice of previously public land is served up to. But in itself, even this should not be a problem – much of the later New Town was built on plans commissioned by private speculators. In the eighteenth and nineteenth centuries there was a relic of feudalism that enforced quality: the Dean of Guild, who had jurisdiction over the construction of new parts of the city. Ellen Meiksins Wood has argued that the unpleasant appearance and shaky civic culture of English cities was a result of the particularly capitalist development of England, its lack of these feudal or guild remnants, along with the more recent lack of the Continent's comparatively strong social democracy. Scotland, conversely, might look 'European' because of its stronger feudal legacies and its stronger working-class movement. Judging by Leith Docks – sorry, 'Edinburgh Harbour' – Scotland has now fully caught up with England.

That's before we even start to consider the Tram that was sup-posed to link the new developments to the city centre, which has been a massively expensive farce, another exemplar of the UK's strange inability to perform even the most basic tasks, to build even the most basic infrastructure. There is really no excuse for this place other than philistinism, stupidity, desperation and graft. The site is now pockmarked with wasteland, and Edinburgh Council ought to be publicly shamed into clawing back some shred of pride by starting over with something that is at least slightly worthy of its location. As it is, there are indications that something might happen here. First, the total commercial failure of much of Leith Docks' redevelopment, left half-constructed, has meant that many of the flats have been let to council tenants, at council rates. That's not an unalloyed good, given that the dwellings are of far lower build quality and space standards than the average council flat. The other interesting thing is that, evidently shaken by their experience in town planning, Forth Ports have talked of reindustrializing the site instead, building wind turbines and a great big biomass power station. It might blow the smell of effluent across Leith, but they could no doubt argue that it was ever thus. In these two fairly grim developments, there are hints of the things that could happen as positive, conscious developments on this site – the return of decent public housing, the reindustrializing and reinvestment in derelict industrial sites. That they're being considered here as a last resort is not necessarily here or there.

The curious subtext of all this is that Edinburgh once managed to assimilate practically every kind of foreign architectural tradition into its streetscape, and made it look convincingly of its place, made it look Scottish. Athenian classicism, French town planning, various forms of Gothic, even 1930s art deco and post-war Brutalism, all can feel utterly local when built here, if done with the right amount of thoughtfulness and conviction. Interestingly, however, Edinburgh's architects couldn't take the pallid pseudomodernism of the New Labour era and assimilate that to the genius loci. At Leith Docks, they merely achieved a highly believable simulation of the Thames Gateway on the Firth of Forth.

Chapter Fifteen

Aberdeen: Where the Money Went

After the Oil Rush

It often escapes attention, especially south of the border, but the UK is an oil state. Although, unlike that riot-torn compendium of inequality, violence and social collapse Norway, the British government had the good sense to leave North Sea Oil in private hands, much money has been generated by the oil deposits off the north-east coast of Scotland, and it should have left some interesting effect on Aberdeen. This former fishing and shipbuilding town has, for over thirty years, been the centre for the administration, exploitation and development of the fossil fuels discovered off the coast of Scotland. So Aberdeen should, in theory, be a pulsating hub of the enterprise economy, it should glitter with gorgeous architecture, vaulting forms and general pugnacity. Full of petrodollars and a large population of 'wealth creators', it ought to be a thumping vindication of British free-market capitalism.

Strained sarcasm aside, it isn't quite that. Aberdeen, when it was a pejoratively thin-lipped Presbyterian town that made its money from fish and boats, had the kind of proper architectural and urbanist ambition so common to Scotland and so foreign to England. Strict building laws, a focused and clear town plan, decent upstanding architecture, all worked together to create a unified, coherent urban identity, facilitated by ready supplies of granite. It is striking, almost dreamlike, to find an entire city made of this stuff; under the slate-grey skies, it is an environment so regionally specific that you could easily get lachrymose. Almost everything in sight is grey. You can just imagine the colourful! architectural contingent, the likes of Will Alsop, Christophe Egret or AHMM, having coronaries in the face of it. 'But where's the *vibrancy*?' In fact, Aberdeen is bustling most of the day, with the colour scheme obviously not having an immediately depressing effect, and in that perhaps traces of the oil money can be seen. It is personable, and by Scottish standards, cosmopolitan. Lost on our arrival at around midnight, dazed after hours upon hours on a train, we were given directions by a group of young men and women out on the town, half West African, half East European. They told us a little about the town, and recommended a wander around Torry, on the other side of the river Dee.

The hypothetical 'European visitor' invoked occasionally on these pages is (here in particular) an *actual* European, my partner Agata. On this, her first trip to Scotland, it was obvious that she felt far more at home than she ever had in the English cities we had walked around. This was the third Scottish city she had seen in a week, and she was already asking why we didn't move here; she couldn't see how anyone in their right mind could ever get excited about Manchester or Brighton when there was Glasgow, Edinburgh and Aberdeen. The gradual realization that the weather was likely to stay like this was, eventually, enough to dampen her ardour, but she'd recognized the fact that city planning was really taken seriously here, and the civic life that it implies is, to a great extent, visible and real, in the present. The problem, and it's a big problem, is that this uniqueness has a particular temporal limit. In Aberdeen, it ends in the mid-1970s, roughly the time that redevelopment ends in, say, Glasgow. Yet while Glasgow's industrial economy fatally contracted in that decade, Aberdeen's surged forth from nowhere, a new petrochemical giant emerging from its granite carapace. The architectural result is identical in both cities.

The central paradox of Aberdeen, which also applies to the UK as a whole, is as follows. When it was a relatively poor town, Aberdeen spent enormous amounts of time and money on architecture and planning; the early-nineteenth-century development of Union Street nearly bankrupted the municipality and its backers. Civic architecture from the 1930s to 1970s shows a correct, if sometimes rather dour municipal standard being kept up. Yet in the thirty-five years since Aberdeen became the Oil Capital of Europe, the city has not seen a single worthwhile building in the city centre. *Not one.* Over a quarter-century of parsimony and mediocrity has been wealth's bequest to the city. In fact, as you soon find if you cross the Dee into the tenements of Torry, *not even wealth has been wealth's bequest to the city.* Maybe for the first few years, until the gold rush calmed down, there just wasn't time – but the most recent proposals and buildings are perhaps the worst of all. That this isn't even *surprising* is indictment enough. How on earth did we settle for this? How did Aberdeen settle for it?

The poverty of architecture in the UK is often, and justifiably, ascribed to industrial decline. The story is the same whether the site is in Wapping, Govan or Digbeth, when it comes to shell-shocked municipalities agreeing to anything that might reinvigorate their moribund economies and generate jobs and investment: fancy architecture can wait, but for god's sake don't put off Persimmon, Tesco or Travelodge. What makes Aberdeen an almost shocking experience is that here there's no decline. There's a port, and it's working all day, with ships and dockers in constant movement. The harbour area reflects that, from the new hotels to the signs in Norwegian in the waterside theme pubs, to the monumentally obnoxious traffic, with endless lines of lorries and the longest pedestrian waiting times imaginable. Unlike the superficially comparable nuclear port of Barrow, it doesn't feel like a strange, securitized graft onto a dying town, but very much a part of it, organically connected to the life of the city. Yet just next to that harbour is a new Ibis Hotel that is every bit as dismal as every other Ibis Hotel in the UK – more so perhaps, because of the way it clumsily spreads itself out across a sloping cobbled street, which terminates in a miserable Vue cinema. Aberdeen's planning department surely knows that Ibis needs them more than vice versa. It can't have come from lack of confidence. Yet the exact same racket is at work here as everywhere else. There is one consolation, perhaps – the Ibis is at least grey. The planning department must have insisted.

Red Vienna, Grey Aberdeen

What the posters here call Aberdeen's 'civic heart' is a thump-ingly exciting place, running off that vivid contrast between the austere rectitude and sparkling surface of the architecture, the sobriety of the planning and the vitality of its street life. Yet like any other city centre it is soon to undergo changes, as the 'REGENERATING ABERDEEN' posters placed on a derelict building make clear. Each of them shows a thin line drawing of a newly rejuvenated square. They beg a question. Regenerating Aberdeen from what, exactly? From what recent period of decline in this highly economically successful city? A few clues to how limited this success might be become apparent, when you find several derelict buildings in the centre. Even then, something strange happens to dereliction in Aberdeen. The pristine granite doesn't really age, but of course things grow on disused buildings here as much as they do everywhere else, so there is the interest-ing spectacle of shrubbery growing out of otherwise sparkling grey stone buildings. The Macintosh department store on Union Street is a case in point, an Edwardian baroque structure with pretty mosaic signage and unsubtle mid-twentieth-century addi-tions, such as a concrete Gothic extension and some very nice external walkways.

Union Street's general standard of eighteenth- and nineteenth-century buildings is impressive, partly for their elegance, partly just for thoroughness and consistency. You quickly find that the tradition of slightly staid but dignified architecture was intelligently continued in the early twentieth century, as in the ghostly neo-Gothic of Alexander Marshall Mackenzie's Marischal College, or his amusingly stolid, neoclassical St Mark's Church. The American classical RBS building on Union Street showed metropolitan flair, using the expanses of glass made possible by steel frames, then sticking precise, machine-detailed Ionic columns onto them in order not to scare the horses. The 1960s municipal buildings, such as the towering office block housing the town hall, are similarly flattered by their material. The only pre-petrol disappointment is Aberdeen Market, its ungentrified interior space clearly very important to the city's sense of liveliness, but architecturally sadly introverted, based on a series of large, windowless grey drums inserted into the cityscape.

This is all very pleasant, but where it gets really interesting is where topography meets engineer. The sweeping Rosemount Viaduct is a classic 'improvement', rising up a steep slope which the architects exploit to its greatest extent, providing corner towers, oriel windows and a jagged skyline. There are (superb)

charity shops on the ground floors, and tenements above – which, while a good piece of urban planning, must also provide strange and cramped rooms, as the building twists and narrows its way up the hill. Follow this row of tenements and eventually you find yourself at a later adaptation of the tenement system, A. B. Gardner's Rosemount Gardens.

This 1930s council scheme (1930s-designed, that is – it was finished just after the Second World War, as is recorded by a plaque and a Saltire Society bauble) is not based on the tenement structure of Scottish cities at all, which means no shops on the ground floor and no streetline; but it also means no unkempt afterthoughts at the back ends, no outside toilets, no division between ornate front to the bourgeois passer-by and an unseemly mess where they aren't looking. Its inspiration is amusingly obvious – it's a delightful mini-Karl-Marx-Hof in granite, copying practically to the letter, albeit on a smaller scale, the precedent of Red Vienna. The Austro-Marxist municipality in the '30s didn't totally reject the tall flats and courtyard structure inherited from the nineteenth century, as did Modernists in Rotterdam, Berlin and Moscow, but instead adapted them, creating a series of 'Hof' buildings, where strong, proud façades were entered through grand archways, leading to public parks and gardens, around which the flats and their entrances were arranged. The sense of warmth and enclosure the Red Vienna style created is clearly appropriate to the ruthlessly dreich climate of Aberdeen. On each of the archways, there's Eric Gill-like sculptures, with fairly simple optimistic symbolism (bare-breasted woman on flying horse, for instance). When you enter, the feeling is of having stumbled into a pocket park, with trees and swings overlooked by the flats' balconies. The form was never directly emulated, but it marks what is surely the most cheering thing about Aberdeen.

High-Rises versus Tenements

Very interestingly, and unusually for a non-new town in Scotland, post-war modernism was of much the same quality as these pre-war flats, although on a far greater scale. In fact, Aberdeen's towers flaunt their size fearlessly, in a mode not entirely dissimilar to the hulking slab blocks of Glasgow. The especially dramatic hilltop Gallowgate estate is a case in point, with maisonettes and then towers stepping upwards from a vigorously modelled car park. There's nothing original in the design, but everything is used with purpose and strength. There are tapered, cubistic pilotis holding up these massive blocks, and two glass walkways strung between them; the concrete frame is clad in rubble panels, with granite set into it. This use of local materials is stirringly effective in Virginia and Marischal Court, on a site just off Rosemount Viaduct – very Glaswegian in their sheer bulk, but far from Glaswegian in their careful use of materials.

Most, if not all of this, can be found in other towers, in other towns, but Aberdeen has stumbled, perhaps via an enlightened use of its surely sizeable tax revenues, on the blindingly bloody obvious. It hasn't treated its high-rise estates as a problem to be solved, via a similarly sweeping measure to that which created them in the first place. Aberdeen City Council has instead treated them as decent housing, to be maintained and looked after. It helped that they had something of a high quality to start with. The building of these towers in the mid-60s was put under the direct control of municipal architect George McKeith, rather than Wates or Wimpey.[13] Because of this there was no system-building, no cheap instant solutions, but in-situ concrete, sharp Corbusian designs, and granite infill that glows beautifully in the (admittedly rare) sun. And as it seemed to work well, they didn't stop – the city council was still building tower blocks to this standard as late as 1985, when the sober, minimal, rationalistic (and squeaky-clean) St Clements Court was built. It's now used as sheltered accommodation, close to the centre and its amenities, with an exhilarating view – the opposite of the tendency to relegate sheltered accommodation to darkened corners.

The puzzle remains. Of course there's more money in this city than most, but the same could be said about London, or Edinburgh, where the record is quite different. It doesn't seem to exactly fit with Aberdeen's other priorities, such as its enthusiastic embrace of the exurban office block and the shopping mall. But somehow, the money went somewhere decent, for once, in the renovation and upkeep of its housing estates – the one time I've

ever really seen the boom's capital evidently invested in the main-
tenance and respect, rather than the clearance and demonization,
of a working class area. This might be that 'Scottish Difference'
again, although a quick trip to the estates of Glasgow would
divest anyone of that notion. But conversely, walk around the
Victorian tenements of Torry, and things are less impressive. The
housing is on a far smaller scale, reflective of the fishing town that
this once was; none of the enormous sandstone enfilades you can
find in Edinburgh, Clydeside or Dundee, but small terraced flats
with little top rooms set into the roof. People are poor here, and
they're often poor in the tower blocks as well. There's a sharper
air in Torry, though, hints of desperate drinking. There are boutiques in amongst the newsagents and the pubs, but you could still
be in a depressed, granite Gorbals while the ships chug in and out
of the dock just adjacent, their wealth never seeming to reach just
a few dozen yards away.

Union Square, Forever

If you walk back from Torry to the centre, you go through
some of the places where the oil money went, most of which
are mercifully confined to the suburbs. There's the oil drums
and petrochemical storage, a series of branded tubes and cyl-
inders next to the narrow river; a drab '70s office block with a
new, even cheaper new glass bit added, which is the offices for
Sodexho, ODS Petrodata, Atkins – a strange mix of engineers
and our usual outsourcing vultures; and further on, the wipe-
clean business-park nonentity of the Bridge View office block. It's
not encouraging. Then you reach Union Square, the city's new
megamall. In the centre of town, just opposite Marischal College,
there's a city council poster of Union Square's surface car park,
its grim exurban-imposed-on-inner-urban expanse in front of
Marks & Spencer, as if they were proud of it. There are two possible entrances – this particular vision of purgatory, and another,
more urban entrance, by Aberdeen Railway Station. Next to this
is a clumsily massed Jury's Inn, but the mall itself commits its
own acts of civic thuggery – namely incorporating and swallow-
ing up part of the railway station, to leave this with a reduced,

unimpressive rear frontage to the street. So much less important, after all. Walk into the thing, and we're in 2002 forever – a wood-lined roof, and great big canary-yellow Millennium Dome columns, marking an axial entrance to Yo! Sushi; globalization's gift to the city of Aberdeen. It is, however, optimistically named – returning to the Regency gesture of naming developments after the Union between England and Scotland.

The real disaster hasn't happened yet. Union Terrace Gardens is a fabulous public space carved out of infrastructural accident, a bowl curving down from a viaduct along a railway track, a magical little place of mature trees, strange steps and courting Goths. It's completely unique in its topography, a park with real terrain, not a mere civic concession. The story of what is happening here is complicated, so I hope not to get it wrong. To my knowledge, there was first a proposal by a local arts group to build a centre into the dip of the park itself, leaving the salient things about it unchanged. This was rejected in favour of a 'city square' project, which would entail building on top of the gardens, creating a flat landscape which had the interesting consequence of lots of space underneath, where a car park and a shopping mall could be placed. This proposal was then blessed with a multi-million contribution by local oil millionaire Sir Ian Wood; but, in order to unite the two ideas somewhat, there was an international architectural competition for this mall-imposed-upon-park. That didn't impress locals, who protested with a 1,000-strong 'picnic-in'. As a space, Union Terrace Gardens is deliberately secluded. It's a model of civic life based on shelter, quiet, and relaxation, none of which tend to involve much shopping (there are three malls in central Aberdeen). It isn't exactly crowded, but the public esteem for something as undemonstrative as this is heartening.

The underground mall that would level the park has been described by its backers as a putative 'cross between an Italian Piazza and a mini-Central Park'. That line sums up what the problem is here: the topographical specificity of the place, the things that make it impossible anywhere else, are to be obliterated. It's hard to imagine a more provincial statement. We could be a great Scottish city, but instead we'll settle for a lesser version of somewhere else. That said, Aberdeen evidently took the 'Central Park' line literally, and so the competition was won by the American architects Diller Scofidio & Renfro, designers of New York's High Line Park, strung across a disused freight railway. Their proposal, entitled 'Granite Web', involves a series of billowing mini-hills which will apparently make the park 'greener', despite obliterating its trees.[14] It may end up being an interesting piece of architecture, although it seems radically unsuited to the local climate. The proposal's most counter-intuitive point, though, is to remove the site's actual topography, and to add some fake hills. The word 'Disney' has been used. Still, it's an impressive amount of hoops to leap through for the purpose of yet another shopping mall.

Chapter Sixteen

From Govan to Cumbernauld:
Was the Solution Worse than the Problem?

The Moral Second City

In his tract *Architecture and Nihilism*, the ex-Marxist theorist and
recent Mayor of Venice Massimo Cacciari makes the claim that
'the Metropolis' cannot be an industrial city. It's administrative,
bureaucratic, financial, cultural. What Cacciari was referring to
was the 'Great Cities' of the early twentieth century, those that
were in the vanguards of science and art – Paris, New York,
London, above all, Vienna. On the face of it this is a counter-
intuitive idea, and not even particularly accurate with regard
to the cities he mentions. It's also odd to hear that Detroit,
Manchester or Shanghai were not metropolitan. What Cacciari's
notion does accurately describe, however, is what sort of a city
would flourish under late capitalism, and what sort would not.
It's also one possible explanation for the genuinely tragic decline
of Glasgow. Not the Second City in population since the 1950s,
Greater Glasgow's population of 1.2 million is only half that of
the Metropolitan West Midlands or Greater Manchester; smaller
even than the Leeds-Bradford West Yorks sprawl. Devolution has
favoured the financial and administrative capital in Edinburgh
more than its much larger neighbour to the west. What is surely
indisputable, however, is that Glasgow was and remains the
architectural, cultural, and, frankly, moral Second City of the
UK. It had a chapter in *A Guide to the New Ruins of Great Britain*,
but as that book and this one aver that it *is* the rightful Second
City, there is no sensible reason, given that Greater London

has four chapters altogether, that Greater Glasgow should not have two.

The two places covered in this journey both have claims to some kind of independence from Glasgow proper. The first is Govan, a medieval town which became a shipbuilding centre in the nineteenth century, being annexed to the Second City of Empire as late as 1912; the second is the New Town of Cumbernauld, which was populated almost entirely by Glaswegian council tenants from its inception in the late '50s to its completion a decade later. Glasgow, like London, sprouted numerous 'overspill' towns planned by the Labour governments to relieve its chronic overcrowding, once among the worst in Europe. Unlike in London, but like, say, in Liverpool, those New Towns have often been held to account for the drastic decline of the city's national and international status. London did not seriously suffer from the creation of Stevenage, Hatfield, Crawley, Harlow, Basildon and Milton Keynes; its population declined only slightly, making up most of the losses by the end of the century; its hegemonic power was not changed, it simply grew a new, better designed commuter belt. That the creation of Speke, Runcorn and Skelmersdale undermined a Liverpool that lost half its population between the '40s and the '90s is more likely. But Glasgow, which was partly diffused into East Kilbride, Livingston, Irvine and Cumbernauld, could surely claim that its power was thus blunted, that its teeming urban density was emasculated, that it was persistently treated and patronized as a 'problem'. London could point at its East End as the locus of poverty and suffering, and emerge otherwise unscathed. Glasgow was damned en bloc, with the notorious post-war Bruce Report seriously advocating demolishing the entire city. The scorn the rest of the country had for it was amply reflected in compulsive self-hatred.

But there was a rather larger process at work, which it would be foolish to deny. Glasgow was among Europe's first cities to reach the one million mark at the turn of the century – along with Vienna, Berlin, Paris, St Petersburg and Moscow – but it was the only one that was not and never had been an administrative, bureaucratic city. It was a bourgeois city, in the sense that it had what its English equivalents such as Manchester conspicuously lacked, a middle class that both lived and invested in it; but it was, more than anything else, based on building stuff and making stuff. The industrial decline of the UK necessarily meant the decline of Glasgow. This is often described as a natural, irreversible process, as though it were unavoidable that the city would decline after lower-wage industrial powers emerged in South East Asia and elsewhere. The decades upon decades of refusal to invest in the city and its industries were not, however, inevitable. The two stagnated in tandem. Research and development in technology and heavy industry continued in the late twentieth century, just largely not in Glasgow. So did investment in public infrastructure. London's Underground transport system, for instance, was expanded further and further from the early twentieth century onwards to touch every new suburb, every Enterprise Zone. Glasgow never even got a second tube line, despite its boundaries and council estates extending further into Renfrewshire and Lanarkshire. So we end up with the current situation where, as is luridly reported in recession travelogues, parts of Glasgow have lower life expectancies than besieged Gaza.

The journey described here is an experiment, an attempt to test a hypothesis. Our title derives from a song by the Pet Shop Boys, 'Twentieth Century', which states a common thesis about that era of revolutions. Very bad things existed, and then very bad things would come to replace them. 'I learned a lesson from the Twentieth Century,' sings the Tyneside chansonnier; 'We threw out what was wicked, and threw out what was good as well.' The chorus runs: 'Sometimes, the solution is worse than the problem ... let's stay together.' It's obvious enough what he means. Communism for one, modernist architecture and planning, for another. Strathclyde is abundant in proofs and refutations of this hypothesis, so we start with Govan, a dense and impoverished shipbuilding district, exactly the kind of place from which people were moved into Cumbernauld. The new town's population was intended to be at least 80 per cent Glaswegian in the 1960s, and many of them would surely have hailed from these tenement-lined streets. What makes it an interesting test case, however, is the fact that Govan is relatively intact. Unlike the Gorbals to its east, or the East End on the other side of the Clyde, it was

not subject to wholesale comprehensive redevelopment in the post-war decades; it had been relatively left alone by 1971, when Taransay Street here was among the first working-class tenement areas to be 'rehabilitated' by the Glasgow Corporation rather than levelled. Most of its tenements remained, as did its pubs, shops, cinemas, institutes and even its once-independent town hall. What did get built was fairly incremental and timid. Govan even has a still-functioning shipyard. So, although the population density and most obviously the employment has changed very drastically, the physical fabric is much the same as it would have been when Glasgow was among the ten most powerful and populous cities in the world. Cumbernauld is also an interesting test case in that it isn't an easy punchbag, but somewhere that won numerous awards in its time, and remains to this day more affluent than many of the working-class districts in Glasgow proper. Solution, meet Problem.

The Speculators' Zenith

The place we start in Govan is Cessnock Subway Station. The Glasgow Subway, under the control of Strathclyde Public

Transport, was recently given a governmental cash injection after a period in which closure was seriously being considered. Not only was this at the same time that Crossrail, DLR extensions and the London Overground were being built in the First City, but also at the time that Glasgow's inner motorway was being belatedly extended, its blue steel-and-concrete flyover now traversing Southside districts with some of the lowest levels of car ownership in the UK. So the Subway survives, still currently with its cute '70s livery and design of brown bricks and curved moulded plastic, entirely intact. That redesign was the last time any real investment was made in high-speed public transport here – just to keep the single line going, never mind extending it. Cessnock, of the same absurdly small proportions as much of the Glasgow underground, has an unusually demonstrative entrance, a square archway with spiky metal outgrowths to deter anyone who might consider climbing it.

The reason we're starting here is that the entrance is built into Walmer Crescent, a development by the architect Alexander 'Greek' Thomson, one of the architects who 'built Glasgow': an internationally influential stylist who took neoclassicism to its limits, creating an intense and robust personal language out of Greek forms that so often lent themselves to mere antiquarianism. Famously, he had never travelled to London, let alone to Greece, though his architectural legacy was taken up as far away as Chicago. Thomson was also a typical Glasgow bourgeois, a keen-eyed property developer, and here he was both developer and architect. Accordingly, Walmer Crescent is a reminder of something now rather hard to imagine – the possibility of property speculation creating coherent, convincing and attractive urbanism, although here as ever in Scotland the feudal legacy should not be discounted. The Crescent itself is harshly cubic in its details, with its masonry cut into rectilinear patterns and recesses, conflicting with the swoop of the curving streetline; the shape and depth of the fenestration contrasts on each level, and the columned top floor, as often with Thomson, is considerably more Egyptian than Greek in its severity. The Crescent is class-segregated, like most Victorian urbanism, with servants' quarters in the basement, but none of it today looks particularly affluent.

The sandstone is handsome but corroding, and in one corner shrubs are growing out of the masonry. This doesn't mask a superbly confident and forthright piece of architecture and urbanism, but reminds you what sort of place you're in.

Coming out of Walmer Crescent, you're in Paisley Road, part of a long artery to the coast, built up by the more workaday kind of speculator. In Glasgow, that's largely a very good thing, at least at our comfortable historical distance. A strongly modelled sandstone sweep takes over here, and doesn't let go. The ingredients are exactly the same as you will find in bourgeois districts like Hillhead – soft sandstone, yellow then deep red, wide and high bay windows, mostly classical details, all on a grid structure of streets, with shops and pubs on ground floors and corners; mostly gardenless, albeit leavened by parks. There are differences, and it would be seriously amiss not to notice them – here the bays are much shallower, the rooms smaller, and the shops and pubs significantly grimmer (although the caffs are almost as good as those near the University). The masonry is also not in the sandblasted, polished and glittering state it can so often be in the West End. As an ensemble, it's still hugely impressive, and the details reward close examination, such as the entranceways to one row of anonymous developers' tenements, which boast rusticated columns that evoke the French utopian architecture of Ledoux.

The corner buildings are often modelled accordingly, pieces of urban punctuation, as at the District Bar pub, where a seemingly classical building bulges upwards into a prickly, columned iron spike. Remember here that in 1919 the government decided that upgrading the quality of beer might help calm the revolutionary ardour of Red Clydeside. I didn't inspect its quality. Around here, the grid starts to offer views of 'iconic' post-industrial, regenerated Glasgow, in the form of two tall, metallic extrusions – the largely ornamental Finnieston crane, the tower of the Glasgow Science Centre, a bow topped with a room for the views. In the foreground are factories. Walk along here for a while, then turn northwards, through Ibrox into the centre of Govan, and these industrial structures start to loom somewhat. The tenements, though, just become even more impressive in their power and elegance, and even more alarming in their state of wear. It's not the satellite dishes that would excite scorn in the West End, it's the discoloured and rotting masonry – needless to say far worse in the non-'architectural' and enduringly grim back-ends of the tenements – but even more than that, the state of the streets themselves. The roads are potholed, grass is growing, and shrubbery emerges in the most unexpected places. Just in the near distance are two of the more elegant Glasgow high-rises, the only two in this part of Govan, both of them in multicoloured brick with glass stairways, a rare example from the spec builders who offered their services and systems to municipalities that doesn't look shameful next to the architectural efforts of Glasgow's nineteenth-century speculators. That the flats inside would have been more spacious, better heated, with toilets, goes without saying.

The point remains, however, that Glasgow's urban fabric is not a great argument for the aesthetics of municipal socialism. The height and elegance of the speculative tenement is here partly supplemented by slightly later reforming efforts. The basic structure is retained, but the differences are very telling, in that they are motivated by humanism and not by aesthetics. You can see them at the corner of Ibrox Street and Whitefield Road. There are three storeys rather than the usual four (to save the back-breaking walks upstairs), no bays but also no basements, and a thin

layer of stone dressing on the frontage, rusticated to make it look more earthy. The pitched roof has not been hidden by a row of battlements or chimneys. There's hedges in front. There's nothing wrong with it, other than the obvious fact that the problem with the earlier tenements – where the look, the public face, was more important than the people living inside – has merely been reversed. Compare them, for instance, with the prospect at the corner of Govan Road and Southcroft Street, where a yellow sandstone block turns the corner with an achingly elegant and modern circular window, leading to a row of skinny red sandstone tenements in enfilade, a melodramatic and memorable vista that could go on for a mile without getting boring. There's a shop on the ground floor, as all the Urban Renaissance documents insisted. A pawn shop.

Nihil Sine Labore

It would be anachronistic to lament much of this, as if you weren't in an area that was built as quick and cheap housing for shipyard workers, crowded in by the ton, with those bays a piddling concession to space in a city where two families to a room was considered acceptable. There is however one obvious absence which helps account for much of the very obvious poverty and decay in Govan, and that's industry, the remnants of which cut a desolate swathe through the residential areas, much as it would have done in the 1890s (so no blaming post-war zoning policies here, thank you). You do see big metal sheds, and sometimes, in amongst the weeds and half-caved-in walls you see things happening in them – Industrial Springs Ltd, vast in corrugated iron with red trim, or Shearer Candles, est. 1897. You also see a lot of obviously unemployed and obviously ill people milling around, waiting for Iain Duncan Smith to procure them a bike for a call-centre job in Edinburgh. That's not to say that Govan hasn't made any attempt to redevelop its industrial sites, as that would be unfair. Weird new-economy colonies are interspersed with the sheds, all of them in a business-park vernacular – yellow brick, red Trespa, fun roofs – that you could find absolutely anywhere, so it's hard to see it as much of a sign of local self-confidence.

Large car parks and in-between spaces stretch alongside. There are few signs, logos or people to help detect what is happening here, nor any notable trace of activity. This, presumably, is the 'Digital Media Quarter @ Pacific Quay', or so says a big sign adjacent.

Your eye is immediately taken by two extremely striking things at this point, two markers of Govan's fluctuating status. Govan Town Hall is on one side. Designed by Paris-trained Beaux Arts architects Thomson & Sandilands in 1897, it's as impressive as the civic palaces of London Boroughs like Lambeth or Woolwich, probably more so. It's a conventional design, without much trace of the innovations or mutations of Glasgow's turn-of-the-century architects like J. J. Burnet, James Salmon or Charles Rennie Mackintosh. What it tries to do is just impress, and it does that amply, with its Roman portico surmounted by Scottish Baronial turrets and an Italian Renaissance dome of especially thumping proportions, all in lush and tactile red sandstone. There are improving quotes on it, such as the Latin legend 'Nihil Sine Labore', or Nothing Without Work, a rather bitter choice of phrase. Govan Town Hall isn't used as a municipal building now, but is instead rented by film companies, who have the most spectacular ready-made set just adjacent should they ever want to make a *Two Nations* film. Just visible through barbed wire on the other side of the road is a place I covered in the previous volume of this work, a dockside regen scheme housing BBC Scotland and the Glasgow Science Centre. I hadn't realized when I visited it that it was in Govan, that this impressive Victorian urban area was just next door – and this can only partly be blamed on my ignorance. There is simply no connection, physical or otherwise.

Walk around the corner from here and central Govan really hits you, and I mean that in the best possible sense. The faintly late-70s futuristic Govan Subway Station is right at its heart, as it should be, and you can be in the centre of Glasgow in no time. That doesn't lessen the sense that this would or could be a great centre in and of itself. There is one fantastic building after another: a medieval church, a Victorian Printworks with a bust of the misnamed 'Guttenberg', among others, a 1930s moderne cinema (which oddly hides its dereliction with a hoarding showing a photograph of it in the 1930s), and commercial buildings of serious vigour and presence, linked intimately and inextricably with more streets of tall sandstone tenements; the whole disposed around a triangular public space where you can sit and take it in. The Pearce Institute is the civic focus for it all, and on the day I visit there's a poster, indicating the evening's topics for discussion. 'Central Govan Tenants and Residents: 1. Housing Association Issues (the entire Glasgow housing stock became a charity case a few years ago). 2. Cuts in Public Services. 3. Policing. 4. Factoring.' These offer a pretty clear picture of what is on Govan's mind.

There has been quite a bit of post-industrial development in Central Govan. There's an '80s shopping mall, not as awful as these usually are, avoiding a complete destruction of the urbanism around it, but its blank red-brick lines were surely more at home in Milton Keynes. Slightly more interesting is a residential extension of the centre based on brick, render and metal tenements. At first, it locks itself onto the existing urban structure, continuing a line of Victorian flats, albeit with an uncomfortable blockiness. When it approaches the Clyde, that structure breaks up, but is replaced with nothing worthwhile – driveways and vague, car-centred spaces for the pedestrian. More interesting is a mini-estate designed by Collective Architecture for the Govan Housing Association, in less clichéd materials: a purply brick that goes well with the red all around, and gold-ish panelling. Like many Housing Association areas it can't clearly decide whether it's a new, public-spirited piece of public housing or an aspirational alternative, aimed at affluent outsiders. That's because it's both. A blocky tower and low-rise terraces work their way reasonably intelligently into the urban fabric, although I'm perhaps being kind because of the contrast with a nearby post-war estate, which is a completely typical example of the sad decline of Glasgow architecture after 1945. Just a series of three-storey, grey-rendered tenements with pitched roofs, vaguely arranged around scrubby green spaces, with nothing either positive or negative in them, a nullity, an entropic zone overbearingly invigilated by CCTV. Whoever commissioned these evidently didn't think they lived in one of the world's great cities; his counterparts at Whitehall would surely have agreed.

Reach the Clyde, and there are two enormous grey sheds, on either side of the river. One of them is the Riverside Transport Museum, a back-of-an-envelope design by Zaha Hadid. Amusingly, the best view of it is offered by a kipple-ridden space just off Govan Churchyard. The river is fenced off, and in front of it there's scrub, a sofa, several cushions, plastic bags, rugs, cardboard boxes, shipping containers, bollards, and some parked taxis. The Museum itself is a remarkable engineering feat tailored to the architect's overweening ego, an ethically neo-Victorian design where a prodigious metal structure is immediately masked by a tinny skein. It's a good place to test the architectural avant-garde's pulse, this, as Hadid's partner Patrik Schumacher has described this kind of digitally-enhanced shed-creation as the logical successor to constructivism – a style as appropriate to post-Fordism as modernism was to the post-war consensus. The up-tick logo of the roofline and the effacement of work and tech-nology is an infuriating exercise in whimsy and vacuity, but the Big Shed typology used here is not inappropriate. It's hard to say the Riverside Museum is alien to the urban context.

Just opposite, on the Govan side, is the last remnant of Govan's shipbuilding, the white and blue steel shed of BAE Systems Surface Ships. Deindustrialization is real enough, but in Glasgow as elsewhere it should not be exaggerated. That this survives at all is the eventual result of one of Red Clydeside's most militant actions, one which is especially relevant during the current crisis – the Upper Clyde Shipbuilders Work-In, in the early 1970s. Edward Heath's government were determined to let 'lame ducks' die, and the under-invested and under-resourced Clyde shipyards were meant to go away quietly, downsized, closed and sold off to the highest bidder. Instead, Communist shop stewards led a 'work-in', to prove that the yards were viable, and even more importantly perhaps, viable under the control of their workers. In that, they presaged the co-operative autogestion movements that took over factories in Argentina last decade. Largely due to the work-in, the shipyards were nationalized and kept going through the 1980s. The shipyard in Govan was privatized in 1988, and inevitably, it's now operated by a subsidiary of BAE, the arms-dealing behemoth that is arguably neoliberal Britain's most successful economic entity. It could be argued that this corporation, formed out of several formerly state-owned bodies and aided by great government largesse, is the logical successor for the Clyde's former industrial expertise. BAE Systems Surface Ships has a revenue of over £1 billion. It's hardly struggling. Yet I've often heard it suggested that the cranes of the old shipyards are what you see above the tenements in Govan, rather than those of a working factory for destroyers and attack ships. Here it all still is, hiding in plain sight. It employs far fewer people, and there's the rub, but you can still see ships being built from the Glasgow Harbour luxury flat development, on the other side of the river. Much as it might still weld together warships, there's not much false consciousness on the part of Govan – the SNP's position on the Iraq war didn't stop them electing its deputy leader Nicola Sturgeon as their MSP.

Modern Boys, Modern Girls, It's Tremendous!

You can, if the trains are running on time, get from here to Cumbernauld in about thirty-five minutes. Subway to Buchanan Street, into Queen Street station, then a short journey through north-east Glasgow and a brief, hard-to-spot 'green belt' and you're in the New Town, the alternative, the putative solution to the problem that was and is Govan and the places like it. There is a cheat involved here. We could take a much more circuitous route to the peripheral estates of the Glasgow Corporation, to Easterhouse or Castlemilk, where we could find the nondescript estate off the corner of central Govan reproduced on an enormous scale; but instead we're going to a place which won every architectural award going, and which was immortalized in celluloid in the dizzy teenage utopia of *Gregory's Girl*, a 1981 film which presents an enormously flattering picture of the town, notably by making sure it never presents an exterior shot of its most famous building. More of that later. Cumbernauld has roughly the same population – around 60,000 – as many of the outlying Glasgow estates, although again, we find a poor argument for local government and democracy.[15] The elected Glasgow Corporation too often created sloughs of despond, formed as if by accident;

the unelected quango that was the Cumbernauld Development Corporation managed to create something that, it is soon evident, was taken very seriously, with great sensitivity clear at every level of the design. That shouldn't have to be true, and in, say, the contrast between the GLC or Hatfield Development Corporation, it wasn't, but here the unflattering difference (you'll have passed Sighthill and Red Road on the train up) is undeniable.

The first sight of Cumbernauld as you exit the rather meek SPT station is intriguing – an axial progression of terraces, with an underpass placed in the middle. The one non-'new' building, a rustic row of shops with a café, is off to the side, but it's as if it has been put there for reassurance. The district nearest the station is called Carbrain, and like most of Cumbernauld it is fairly low-rise. Cumbernauld was a 'mark two new town', so it took into account the criticisms that were applied to the Attlee government's efforts, from Stevenage to East Kilbride, which were thought too dispersed, too suburban, too monofunctional. The other major 'mark two' town is Milton Keynes, a place specifically designed so that you could drive through it without noticing, with nothing originally allowed to be taller than the tallest tree – a faintly psychotic way to design a town, though frequently rather elegant if you get out of the car. Cumbernauld wisely didn't go as far as this, but it introduced a road system that presaged its Buckinghamshire relative, where the pedestrian does not at any point have to cross a road, and the driver never has to wait at a traffic light. To your right is a row of six-storey tenements, with a svelte pedestrian bridge protruding from them. They're in what you soon find is the dominant Cumbernauld material, brick with grey render, which unfortunately is usually stained or otherwise discoloured. At the roof, the brick takes over, forming around curious semicircular windows. There's snow on the ground. It feels a little bit like the outskirts of Kiev.

In front of you, however, is the signposted route to the town centre, so it is in this direction that we proceed. A greensward surrounds the underpass, with long grey terraces rising one after another, on a hill. Within a few minutes you've already seen more greenery and felt more space than you would in an hour in Govan, and evidently that was the point. The underpass itself has been 'designed', with faceted little panels, and it's very wide and spacious. The houses display a design which at first it's hard to decide is clever or stupid. They're again in grey render on brick, they have pitched roofs, and they are very, very small, albeit with larger windows than the Glasgow municipal norm. To the back of each row is a garage, though cars are still parked in the street. But why, you wonder, have they basically recreated the Victorian terrace on an even smaller scale? Just outside of Glasgow, of all places? Soon you notice two clever things. Each terrace on the hill has been arranged with its neighbour, above and below, in mind. Every view upwards or downwards is surprising, with odd angles and views of the hills just outside the town. The pedestrian principle is especially pleasing here, with the whole thing unmarred by the slightest hint of traffic. Then you notice the landscaping, which is heavy, great big cobbles of rubble set into all the places you're not meant to walk, but without resorting to fences or spikes; occasionally with boulders dropped onto them. A wonderful way to design something this simple – we'd rather you didn't step here, but if you're going to, we won't stop you. And immediately, the craggy, mountainous, northern topography has been taken into the design of the most basic built fabric.

The absence of certain things you see a lot of in Govan starts to become felt. There are no shops, by which I don't just mean a lack of bookies and pawn shops, but of any shop at all. No pubs, either. I stumble instead onto a Free Church, a modern design in wood and harling that doesn't appear to have been touched since 1975, with very neat typography. Up to this point I've been following the signs to Cumbernauld town centre, but then the route is blocked by a new development of exurban-looking houses in closes, and the sign doesn't have anything to say about this. So I try to skirt it, passing another, bigger church, again of very modern design, and a secondary school, and a heart-in-mouth view of the ensemble billowing downwards. After a while of this I worried I might end up getting terminally lost here, so retraced my steps and took another route entirely (the earlier sign was more permissive), through a park.

There was a townscaper of genius at work here. The landscape architect of Cumbernauld was one G. P. Youngman, and much of what made this walk especially enjoyable can be put down to his talents. A winding pedestrian path weaves through what you abruptly realize is not, in fact, a park at all, but what Cumbernauld has instead of streets – hillocks on each side, a wooden walkway, thickets of trees. You could be in a nature reserve, or one of those BedZed-style eco-buildings extruded out to form a town, but you definitely couldn't be on a street. This, in theory, is bad. Streets encourage life and stuff. Take away proper streets, and chaos and mugging apparently ensues. Yet I saw as many people on this path as I did on Govan Road, and they didn't look especially menacing, although one told me I wouldn't find much to photograph round here. That Glasgow municipal self-esteem problem moved here, too.

The houses vary wildly in their treatments, although they were all designed of a piece, by the development corporation. Their lead architect, Hugh Wilson, was co-creator of the Arndale Centre in Manchester, but like his partner, Sheffield Municipal Architect Lewis Womersley, he deserves better than to be remembered for it. The two architects seemed to share a great deal – the only place I've been that combines such total modernity with intense local and topographical specificity to this degree is the Gleadless Valley in Sheffield. The houses, now, are less neo-back-to-back than those downhill. They've got gardens, but they also look more modern and more crisp. Some are worn and almost derelict, some in fine nick, with no obvious pattern as to why and wherefore, no obvious slum area or affluent area (that, too, was deliberate). Right to Buy obviously hit Cumbernauld fairly hard. Perhaps the only real caveat about this place is that it'd be a little tricky for the unfit, and I find myself slightly out of breath from all the ups and downs. At the underpass, stairs go up to a bus stop, but not to a road; pass through and you're finally at the town centre.

Adapt and Destroy

Now, if it weren't for three grey tower blocks in the near distance, you really could be in Milton Keynes, but for the aggressive Strathclyde-in-January weather. That careful urban structure you've just walked through is replaced with a large surface car park. The landscape has gone from being fascinating and unique to being a landscape that you have seen in a million different places, a million times. Retail sheds on the motorway; a Tesco Extra, with another even bigger car park in front; a PFI college, with a Blair Hat on top; a covered shopping mall. The golden arches look out over all of it, and for the first time so far, you spy a CCTV camera. There are other things, more clearly of the era, to be seen. Non-avant-garde modernism is represented in offices for Lanarkshire Council, low-rise and smart, and a larger, vaguer brown brick block; the avant-garde are represented in another college building, a worn but imaginative and clear Brutalist cruiser designed by Andy MacMillan and the late Isi Metzstein. Clever bits of landscaping and pedestrian routing can be found in amongst all the subtopian vagueness, but really, you're clutching at straws. Its contrast with the centre of Govan, never mind the centre of Glasgow, is in no way flattering. So how, you would be right in asking yourself, did this end up being the centre of a town which up till now appeared so sensitively and thoughtfully designed?

Cumbernauld town centre was originally supposed to be one single building, of a sort. Its designer, Geoffrey Copcutt, proposed for the site a 'megastructure', which was to rise out of the topography as a great rocky outcrop. Megastructures were a mid-1960s Big Idea, a rearrangement and radicalization of modernism into huge, allegedly adaptable and extendable organisms that provided all the density, diversity and life so palpably absent from many of the more Platonic modernist showpieces. Habitat '67 in Montreal is probably the most famous; the Brunswick Centre and arguably the Barbican in London show traces of it, as does Castle Market in Sheffield. Japanese architects specialized in megastructures for a while. There's an obvious problem with them as theory, which is the combined attempt to provide a clear and legible image in a fixed and heavy material, usually reinforced concrete, and at the same time provide something light, adaptable and changeable; but if managed well enough there is no reason why a megastructure should not work. Shopping mall owners may not be the ideal clients for such an entity.

So Copcutt's town centre was built to include pubs, libraries,

welfare centres, restaurants, nightclubs, bowling alleys, shops, bus station, offices, and had a row of penthouses at the top. The architect intended a few other things too, which never quite came to pass: there was apparently 'a mosaic of sites I had tucked in for flea-markets'[16] in there somewhere, as well as space for hotels. You now realize that the absence of pubs and shops in the residential areas was not entirely stupid, as the entire town was planned round this place, with the intention that nowhere would be more than a fifteen-minute walk from its metropolitan bustle. When pondering it, you have to keep in mind the Apollonian grids of most post-war New Towns, their clear and neat pedestrian precincts without much in the way of drama, complexity or conflict. You have to think of a rainy day in Billingham, as that's the sort of thing the architects had in mind as what they wanted not to achieve. Nonetheless, the main event, as in any New Town, was evidently the shopping, and it's that which caused the downfall of Copcutt's idea. If it was a shopping mall, and an unsuccessful one at that (at first), then it was to be judged on those terms. For that he cannot quite be blamed; although the choice of bare concrete in weather like this was perhaps unwise, if not without a certain craggy grandeur.

All this at first is fairly academic, as walking round the car parks in the town centre you can't at first find any trace of Copcutt's original building – the structure which won 'worst building in the UK' awards for a decade or more, the place memorably described in the Poujadist television spectacular *Demolition* as 'a concrete spaceship from the planet Crap'. It's hard to hide a building this big, but they've almost succeeded. You have to walk to the corner between the blank, pink-walled Antonine Centre (the Roman Wall ran nearby) and the typically sub-Foster Tesco Extra, where you'll see it just above the service areas and the lorries, the long row of porthole-windowed penthouses raised up on one prodigious piloti. They're still inhabited, apparently. It's infinitely more interesting than the shopping centre and the supermarket as a work of architecture, though its ferocity is hard to deny. Walk up some stairs, miraculously still public, and the sight is genuinely shocking. It's like a concrete shanty town, with a series of seemingly random cubic volumes 'plugged in' to the larger structure, all of them in a drastic state, their concrete frames with brick infill looking half-finished, which alarmingly may have been intentional. One of these pods has a little doorway into a branch of William Hill, which is possibly the single bleakest thing I have seen in composing this book. After that, you realize where you are – the service areas of the building, so at the point where glass walkways carry pedestrians, and the only reason for you to be here is to wait for a bus. Walk into the bus station, and the surfaces are lined with mosaic and tile, and you realize that somewhere hidden in all this is a space designed with as much love and intelligence as the housing around it. It's damned hard to see it, underneath all that has followed since.

This, again, is in some ways the fault of the original idea. Those walkways are passing into a row of long, featureless and windowless sheds, the kind of ultra-rationalized non-architecture that the strongly modelled and sculptural skyline of the original town centre building is clearly trying to stop in its tracks, to eliminate before it destroyed architecture as a discipline entirely. Copcutt must have realized that the most truly adaptable buildings, those capable of transforming themselves with the same speed as society and production were transforming in the 1960s, were Big Boxes, where partitions inside and walls outside could be fabricated, removed, moved and expanded with great ease. His move, and the megastructural move more generally, was to try and create a form of building that could do all of those things and still be as vivid, interesting, diverse and architecturally pleasing as the historical city, without of course reproducing it. They must have seen themselves as a last line of defence, and in a sense they were, and that's how we ended up with Zaha Hadid's Riverside Museum. The sheds swallow up the architecture here, that's for sure, but they also prove the original building's capacity for adaptation, as they all are still part of the same organism, still all connected. Inside, there's not much to feel optimistic about. This intrinsically adaptable building has indeed been adapted, as was intended, just as it has been expanded. The original high ceilings were lowered to the usual shopping mall level, with the usual '80s fibreglass neoclassicism all around. There are several different pound shops.

One aspect of the original design that surely hasn't changed is the occasionally baffling complexity. Like many cities (but unlike Glasgow), the structure and plan is completely illegible to the outsider, and the map placed to 'help' the pedestrian is more than slightly terrifying. After a while, you realize there are at least three malls here. One is Copcutt's original, with its narrow, arcade-like structure, which might once have been enjoyable; another, slightly later, a big box with a space frame roof; and then the new Antonine Mall. This is reached via a weird and empty passageway, with nothing but beige walls for company until you come to an enormous mock-Victorian clock, screened off by a glass wall in case anyone would want to vandalize it. I felt like having a crack myself.[17] The shops here are nicer, cleaner, proper normal retail chains like you would get in a normal mall. Next, Costa, Dunnes. After this I walk out and get completely lost trying to exit the complex. Copcutt's scheme, its majesty and folly still palpable, looms proudly out over the car parks and the mess, and then you find yourself at another entrance, a glazed atrium of classic 2000s form (wavy roof, Wetherspoons and all). Next to it are statues: 'The Shopper', from 1981, by Bill Scott, presents a mother and baby in bronze. She looks lost too. After lots of wandering, I get out, to somewhere every bit as gorgeous as the area I'd found myself in on my way to the shopping centre.

Scotland, Scandinavia

Maybe it's the relief at finally finding my way out of the town centre, but I don't think so. The northern suburbs of Cumbernauld are glorious, an architectural triumphal march that doesn't stop until you eventually wind your way back to the town centre (it is, after all, built like that). You take some stairs up onto a ridge. A path leads off it, lined thickly with trees – a forest planted just next to the town centre, coursing between the estates. The tall trees are then dispersed across an area of houses spilling down a valley, all with gently pitched roofs, and tightly planned pedestrian paths running through them – again, you can pass through several 'streets' without having to cross a road. There's a little modernist church, in slightly better condition than the one in Carbrain, though there's still something unpleasantly Temperance or philanthropic about the way Cumbernauld's residential areas are planned around parish churches rather than pubs, cafés or leisure centres. There's a school just next door, a straightforward ribbon-windowed box. The houses are geometrically organized, with weatherboarded links between pebble-dashed masonry, but not in the sense of subsuming everything into a pattern, so much as informal, pretty, even. Three tower blocks in the distance lie beyond a concrete underpass, detailed in a raw *béton brut* that fits perfectly with the roughness of the landscape and the landscape architecture. Passing under it feels entirely logical, a pathway under a main road than doesn't even feel like an underpass. It is a feat to design infrastructure with such a degree of seeming informality and ease. There are new, mid-rise blocks of flats just by the underpass; architecturally, their mild-modernism is fairly appropriate, but the most obvious difference has been the collapse of these carefully, ingeniously planned in-between spaces. They're just blocks with car parks in front. Wasn't that what the 1960s was blamed for?

Through all this you're walking downhill, and at the bottom of the hill is Seafar, an estate of tower blocks and terraces. The three towers are in exactly the right place, enhancing the already vivid sense of enclosure and warmth in this woody, bosky area. They too are arranged around a car-parking area, although there the similarities end. The New Town was designed with the assumption that each household would own a car, and whether we consider that a good thing or not, Hugh Wilson and the town's architects tried to achieve the seemingly impossible – to design a dense, coherent, non-suburban town that had a huge amount of car parking while being accessible and pleasant for the pedestrian. So the parking is arranged into a circular concrete garage, like a crescent of bungalows for vehicles. That's not the most impressive thing – what takes over here is Youngman's landscaping at its most crazy and baroque – the winding path round the garages to the towers has at its edges a sculptural sweep of raised cobbles, so organic and bulging that it looks more like an abstract sculpture than a type of paving. Truly, Cumbernauld boasted the Gaudi of pavements.

Turning left from the towers, there's a development of terraces, again stepping sharply down the valley; in between there is bosky, Nordic planting. The grey and brown houses look completely of this landscape, completely of their place, without at all evoking any specific Scottish form of architecture, neither baronial castles nor tenements. The paving is set at angles down the hill, with the cubic, Bauhaus-Caledonia houses set at angles, with bushes at the corners. Thin trees rise out of them. These communal green strips are again demarcated by melodramatic landscaping – more boulders crashed down here and there, as a small reminder not to walk on them that doesn't need 'keep off the grass' signs. Walk up the hill a little bit and you can see snow-capped mountains in the near distance. There's a small plaque at the end of one of the terraces: 'Saltire Society Award for Good Design, 1963'. It's not unusual to find old Civic Trust plaques on neglected, rotting post-war buildings, but though a *Wallpaper** reader might blanch at some of the porches and additions made by residents to their terraces, surely this place has been used in exactly the manner in which it was intended. The contrast with the town centre is over-whelming. How unusual that it's working-class housing rather than a shopping centre that best represents the place's local pride.

Walking back towards the town centre, the houses lie more dramatically into the landscape, with especially steep pitched roofs set in rows. The town centre buildings look marginally less horrible from this angle, less subtopian, with at least some hint of the original ideas, where you see Copcutt's concrete extrusions passing over a main road with another small, conservative modern church next to it. From here, an underpass to Kildrum, another of the 1960s areas of the New Town. The underpass offers views of some typical Cumbernauld employers – Fujitsu, the Inland Revenue, both evidently taking advantage of the low rent and motorway connections, much as they would in Stevenage. Like most New Towns, Cumbernauld was built up largely, if not exclusively, with council housing, but either employment patterns or the Right to Buy has made much of it look unexpectedly affluent; turn your eye back to the view of the town centre, though, and it's hard to credit it. The worn concrete megastructure and its big-box parasites look drastically sick. The underpass is, like the rest of the landscaping, designed in a heavy, rustic, organic pattern, filtering the pedestrian under the motorways to the centre with great tectonic gusto. Then you're at another series of terraces placed downhill. This time, the clipped modern designs and the density of wintry trees seriously evoke a northerly version of what we'd seen at New Ash Green. There are bungalows off the main pathway, under the trees. There are worn but elegant metal shelters along the road adjacent, with cars parked in them. At the end of it, the underpass to the next estate has taken the organicism to comic heights – a gaping maw, a practically medieval archway. By this point I've gotten myself lost again, and ask for directions. I'm told, kindly enough, that if I don't know the town I'd be better off taking a bus. The bus stop is out of service.

So I decide instead to go for another walk, to test the theory that everywhere is no more than fifteen minutes from the town centre. Forest paths lead to a striking, verdigris-clad factory. Then, uphill, more houses with steep pitched roofs and bulkily landscaped pedestrian paths, their peaks and falls accentuating the drama of the topography. There are new additions in between, in a nondescript suburban vernacular, again punctuated by nothing but car parks, but it's small enough to ignore. Through the town centre again (quicker than I had expected, evidently it's not *that* hard to get used to) and walked back to the station through Carbrain, with more elegant, dense housing that seems to have gone to seed faster than most of the rest of the town. At Greenfaulds Crescent, you find the only part of the New Town that seems to have followed a 'normal' street pattern, with cars parked on a street with houses facing each other on either side. It doesn't seem any more or less successful than the rest of it, despite being the only part that contemporary town planning wisdom would consider sensible or even feasible.

The paradox of Cumbernauld is how such a well-kept and cap-tivating residential town can have allowed its town centre to have become such a subtopian horror. That might be to do with the basic vagueness of the New Town idea in the first place. If it's seen, as it easily could be, as a far-northern suburb of Glasgow, then it doesn't matter so much that central Cumbernauld is a dis-aster; if it's seen as the heart of a distinct town with its own identity (something it undoubtedly possesses), then the absence is a very serious urban defect. Did it 'solve' the problems of Victorian Glasgow, though? It certainly avoided every possible urban pattern of Glasgow, without the slightest trace of the tenement tradition, and without the tiniest hint of the Chicago-style metropolitan brashness of the Second City; but, unlike most of Glasgow's own estates, Cumbernauld replaced what it destroyed with something positive, something with its own pattern, its own locality. There's no reason why both can't peacefully coexist. Not that the New Town should be seen as some admirable but misguided experiment. About halfway through my walk through Cumbernauld, I realized I'd only seen anything similar on the outskirts of Stockholm, where forests and lakes are interspersed with sensitive, cleverly landscaped working-class housing. Given that the Scottish Nationalist left like to hold up the surviving Welfare State consensus in Norway or Sweden as their exemplar for the Scottish Republic (as opposed to other feasible comparisons, like Ireland or Iceland), that's very apt. Here is a New Town which looks on brief acquaintance like an exceptionally successful piece of social democratic, Scandinavian urbanism, a place that an Alvar Aalto or a Sven Markelius would recognize as kin. Its mistakes are obvious, and rectifiable. We could imagine it becoming a model for the new settlements of an independent, leftist, intensely local Scotland. Though England may face a Tory hegemony forever when Scotland secedes, it's hard not to wish them luck.

Chapter Seventeen

Belfast: We Are Not Going Away

From our Foreign Correspondent

Ireland, of course, is not Britain. The *Morning Star* newspaper always runs reportage from Belfast with the proviso 'from our foreign correspondent'. Belfast has a place in a book which claims to deal with 'urban Britain' only in the sense that it's still part of the United Kingdom of Great Britain and Northern Ireland, so any reader who is irked by its inclusion should bear in mind that it is used on these strictly limited grounds. And no offence is intended when I say that the first feeling when in the Northern Irish capital is one of intense familiarity, and that after two visits, that feeling stuck. Intense familiarity is an understatement, in fact. Belfast appears as a place which has faced every single one of the problems that have beset British cities for the last half-century. Depopulation of the inner city and ballooning of exurbs, drastic deindustrialization, the favouring of the car and hence neglect of public transport, ring roads that brutally sever the poor from the centre, furiously divided communities, walls, fences and gates around residential areas, 1980s riverside Enterprise Zones, post-1997 redevelopment of ex-industrial space into cultural centres and luxury apartments, rise of the inner-city shopping mall, urban riots ... Belfast has been subject to every one of these, to a ferocious degree. The curious thing is that it has suffered them for entirely different reasons, at least on the face of it.

Guilty Labour voters in the 2000s in the UK would often mull over the reasons why they were putting their 'x' where they were, and come up with a short list. 'The minimum wage ... working families tax credit ... Sure Start ... oh yeah, and peace in Northern Ireland.' A Tory Party occasionally known as the Conservative and Unionist Party was never going to be able to achieve the latter, but Blair (or rather, Mo Mowlam with a bit of last-minute grandstanding from Peter Mandelson) did genuinely appear to end three decades of low-intensity civil war. As a measure of that success, in a few years Provisional IRA weapons were handed in, Ian Paisley and Martin McGuinness were sharing jokes, the RUC no longer officially existed, and everything was apparently going to get back to normal, whatever that might be. At this distance, you have to go back and read anything written between the 1920s and the 1990s to realize just how completely unexpected this outcome would once have seemed. Obviously, most of us thinking this thought while going to the polls hadn't ever been to Northern Ireland (I certainly hadn't), gave barely a damn about whether it stayed part of the UK (it's hard to imagine any British government not reliant on Unionist support caring much), and experienced it only via the mainland bombing campaigns of the early-to-mid-90s, on much-loved landmarks like Canary Wharf and the Manchester Arndale. As Patrick Keiller notes of his wandering Londoners in 1992, *they didn't seem to think that what was happening in Ireland had anything to do with them.*

All that said, when talking about Belfast, and Belfast's built fabric, it would be crass to simply take aim at the mess it has made of itself, as if it hadn't relatively recently recovered from three decades of urban warfare. It's possible that buildings like the Waterfront Hall, St Anne's Square or the Obel Tower genuinely symbolize to many people here the fact that they can now walk the streets with any but the most residual fear of car bombs, let alone routine assassinations and beatings. The Phoenix-from-the-Ashes public art is as bad here as everywhere else, if not worse, but different criteria surely exist when a city really has emerged from what Belfast has emerged from. All that said, with all those caveats ... Belfast remains an extremely unnerving, disconcerting and disturbing city, a nightmarish vision of what most British cities could quite easily become, what lies just around the corner for them. That vision is taken out of a context in which it's actually an improvement, to be sure – so that should be borne in mind in what follows.

A Colonial Composite

Belfast looks at first like a 'regenerated' northern English industrial city, and a very impressive one. It's bigger and grander than most, proud and demonstrative in its architecture – a Leeds or even a Manchester, rather than a Preston or a Wakefield. Initial acquaintance shows a city a great deal more familiar, in fact, than anything in Scotland or even much of Wales. This might be because it's the protracted consequence of an annexation and a plantation, unlike the relatively equitable Unions with the UK's other two Celtic countries. That is, it's colonial: something supported by the astounding scale of Belfast City Hall, an Edwardian baroque municipal palace of stupendous grandiosity and bulk, centred around an immense Wren-like dome, comparable with the colonial administrative cathedrals of New Delhi, Mumbai or Durban (the latter was apparently an exact copy). The architect, Alfred Brumwell Thomas, specialized in these civic monstrosities, designing versions for Stockport and Woolwich, but neither is as massive and overpowering as this. As a piece of urban planning, it's as authoritarian as can be, but not ineffective. Central Belfast is a gridiron, like those other Victorian shipbuilding centres Glasgow and Barrow, and City Hall is placed right at the heart of it. Around it, in Donegall Square, are commercial buildings that emulate its scale, insurance offices in the most pompous and invigorating twilight-of-empire fashion.

That's not all that looks familiar – in fact, combined colonization by the English and the Scots seems to have brought a certain amount of equal importation from each. Belfast's earlier incarnation as Linenopolis, a textile centre to rival those of Yorkshire and Lancashire, has left several Ruskinian red-brick/Venetian warehouses and mills in the centre. In the south of the grid, their height, their intense colour, and their sheer walls give a dramatic effect reminiscent of Whitworth Street in Manchester or Little Germany in Bradford. There's a lot of infill that mostly follows the height and streetline, hotels and office blocks of little

imagination but which don't disrupt the effect. The turn-of-the-century shipbuilding metropolis has left buildings that could easily have escaped from the Glasgow grid, classical and baroque structures in red sandstone imported from Dumfries. There's a fine progression of them in one corner. The first, on a dramatic corner site, is Bank Buildings, designed in 1900 by W. H. Lynn (designer, as we've seen, of Barrow Town Hall) – sandstone on a steel frame with wide, protomodernist plate-glass windows, a building that many a British city would be envious of, that wouldn't look out of place on either Buchanan Street or Piccadilly, currently with the exalted status of housing Primark. The Central Library, almost next door and also by Lynn, is similarly Glaswegian in its strongly moulded sandstone classicism; then the Leeds-esque mills take over again. Some of the more dignified classical buildings in the centre, such as Hamilton Street or the Custom House, evoke the disciplined eighteenth-century planning of Dublin, as if to redress the balance.

The second half of the twentieth century has granted Belfast a similar bequest to other towns that got rich on heavy engineering and textiles. There's a slightly too sober but very well-made bank by BDP, who kept an office here throughout the Troubles; there's a good Festival Style block with Scando patterns and zigzag balconies, and there's a few not especially interesting speculative office blocks, rightly proud and soaring but devoid of ideas or expressiveness. The comparisons cease to be with northern England and western Scotland by this point, they're more with Birmingham. Belfast's 1980s and 90s buildings are masonry structures on concrete frames, in the sort of blocky, rather coarse postmodernism that you see so often in the centre of the official Second City. At times, when walking round some of the more extensively redeveloped central districts, it's only the weather and the mountains in the near distance that remind you you're not in the West Midlands, or in the more historic areas, the West Riding. The geography, at least, is very local.

By the second day in Belfast you start to register something different in the centre. A 1980s building like the BBC's Northern Ireland department, designed in 1984 by the BBC's in-house architects, employs what to the untrained eye might look like a standard piece of postmodernist vernacular, albeit with art deco rather than Victoriana as the inspiration for its rectilinear mannerisms. Then you gradually realize you're looking at a blast wall, at a structure expressly designed to withstand car bombs. There are many approaches to this problem. The Europa Hotel, bombed an impressive twenty-seven times, is from a distance a fairly normal V-shaped mass of commercial modernism, but up close it's hard to avoid the weird Vegas-like vestibule: a series of bizarre columned spaces which must either have doubled as a screen against bombs, or been imposed as a celebration of the fact that there aren't any bombs any more. You don't see much built in glass until pretty recently, for obvious reasons. The earliest is BDP's 1991 Castle Court shopping mall, a somewhat Richard Rogers-ish piece of bulky high-tech, with ornamental steel frame and a strangely placed short brick wall blocking off one side of it. It's not until my second visit that I realize that here I was walking obliviously past the city centre's only 'peace line'. The most confident postwar (the recent war, that is) structure is Victoria Square, again by BDP, a complex which is a comprehensive redevelopment by any other name. Much of it is taken up by a shopping mall with a large glass dome, to complement those on Donegall Square, with what must have been intended as a hint at the Reichstag and the post-Wende rhetoric of non-ideological 'transparency'. There's pseudo-public access through, and a superb view from the top of the dome. The scheme expands round the street to encompass some inner-city urban regen housing, in the form of a long street block with a tall tower. The architectural language is about right, a slightly Brutalist, vigorous red brick, although the jagged roof is a very early-2000s mannerism. It's not that hard to make a transparent shopping mall; a transparent law courts is a different problem. The Laganside Courts, opened in 2002, were designed by Hurd Rolland; their website claims they are 'one of the leading national practices in the law and order sector'. The building has a conspicuous lack of any but the tiniest windows, which suggests that certain things are not changing. There's a supergrass trial in progress on my second trip here.

Our Legacy, Your Future

Towards the River Lagan, there's a very nice juxtaposition. On one side, the Victoria Clock Tower, a leaning Gothic folly that, local drollery notes, 'has both the time and the inclination'. Opposite is the city centre's best post-war building, J. J. Brennan's Transport House, a tower and wing clad in green tiles with a magnificent constructivist mosaic running down the façade depicting ships, cranes, and robotic workers marching towards the socialist future that evidently didn't come to pass, in an era where the biggest workers' action was the sectarian syndicalism of the Ulster Workers' Council strike in 1974. As a reminder of ideals that have had purchase here at certain times – from the United Irishmen in the 1790s to the solidarity strikes with Red Clydeside in 1919 – it's not just an interesting building, it's an important one. Transport House was occupied until recently by the T&G's successor Unite, who should be ashamed for abandoning this building; the thought of them now occupying some business park in 'Greater Belfast' is faintly heartbreaking.

Walk on a bit from here and the grid's coherence is replaced by the mess of speculation. That's especially sharp where the Westlink slices across the city, an urban motorway comparable in its destructive effect to the M8 more than the Westway, leaving a straggling landscape in its wake. It takes trains as well as cars at one point, which makes it feel even more weird and futuristic, with both crossing each other at angles. Under its riverside flyover you have a series of more or less derelict workshops, a basketball court, and a fence. In the distance is the New Lodge Flats, an estate of towers that recently featured in a Rihanna video, of all things. Each zigzag roof is marked by a portrait of a Republican hunger striker, though that wasn't so clear on MTV Base. The fence itself carries a partially defaced graffito, where certain letters have been meticulously crossed out. It reads: '----- G------- HAS TO ANSWER --- ---- ----'. Local artist Daniel Jewesbury, showing me around, informs me this previously read 'BARRY GILLIGAN HAS TO ANSWER FOR THIS LAND', and refers to the chairman of the Northern Ireland Policing Board, who is also a director at property developers Big Picture Developments.[18] He has to 'answer for this land' because it was zoned as social housing. In 2010, in his other job as policing adviser, Gilligan was allegedly asked by a Housing Association to advise on a 'design issue'; then his company snapped up the land, outbidding the Housing Association.

Visible from here at one point is the St Anne's Square, a development designed by neoclassicist John Smylie. It's a ridiculous building, an ill-proportioned neo-Georgian car park that becomes an enclosed 'Palladian' courtyard, with detailing so cack-handed it makes Paternoster Square look like Aldo Rossi. Whatever else might be said about their recent architecture, it's hard to imagine Birmingham or Glasgow standing for this. A short distance from here and you're in Laganside, the obligatory riverside brownfield Disneyland. It's the same as any other 1980s Enterprise Zone, a Cardiff Bay or a Salford Quays, operated by a quango outside of local government control, with a tamed river created by a concrete weir whose slightly Thames Barrier-like forms make it probably Laganside's best building. The possibility of extending inner Belfast's coherent, legible grid was either rejected or never even considered, so the place is a collection of disconnected towers from different eras.

Era One, the BT tower and the Hilton Hotel, is still fortified, stock-brick-clad with ground-floor blast walls. The post-Good

Friday agreement Era Two is more optimistic, its spec residential towers boasting lots of glass and extraneous bits and bobs, like The Boat flats' brightly coloured picture frames, randomly hung onto the curtain wall. Like a lot of 2000s buildings, it's going to look interesting when the cladding starts falling off. The domed Waterfront concert hall is a tad more civic, but turns its back on the river. There's a twin-tower job in blue glass, left derelict after the financial crash that beset the south of this island even more than the other one. On the ground, Laganside is chaotic, with no coherent riverside walk. Public art entails a sprite-like steel maiden holding up a ring, or an arch, or something, at the entrance to the city from the river. This place has some sort of record for nominations to *Building Design*'s Carbuncle Cup award. In 2010 alone were put forward The Boat and Broadway Malyan's Obel Tower, the tallest building in Ireland (the best of this bad bunch, to be fair, as its east façade has some grace), plus St Anne's Square. The latter was surely robbed of victory only by the fact none of the judges had seen it first-hand. Just before it was wound up, the Laganside company put up a panel listing its achievements, with the chilling words used in the heading to this section above. The abiding impression of familiarity is not in any way dispelled by the fact that every architectural change can be related to a change in the level of conflict; as it would be, in a city where every new development between the mid-70s and the 2000s had to receive the specific approval of the British Army. The fact remains that in London, Birmingham or Manchester you can equally find a 1980s–90s brick-clad postmodernism giving way to a confident, glazed new modernism from the late '90s onwards, seemingly solely due to changes in architectural fashion. Exactly the same thing, for apparently different reasons.

Ulster Defensible Space Association

What is described above is not so extreme, not so unusual. Stick to the centre and the only disturbing thing about the Belfast landscape is the lowest-common-denominator approach to redevelopment; its sins are the sins of other cities. Things are different once you go beyond the ring road. Drastically so. Inner Belfast,

conveniently due to the Westlink, is demarcated by a cordon sanitaire of wasteland and surface car parks, with the odd marooned
terrace of Victorian houses. It just serves to make the change more
glaring. It's not the most obvious barrier, though, in a city which
has in one estimation forty-eight 'peace lines'. The most famous
of these is in West Belfast. The Shankill and Falls are a very short
walk away from the centre, but the scarred spaces you have to go
through to get there make it seem considerably longer. The road
leads you over a very, very busy motorway, and then a jolly little
angel with outstretched arms on a plinth informs you that you
are entering the Shankill. The low quality of Belfast public art
has its reasons, it's soon clear – best to keep it neutral. When you
first see the Loyalist Murals in the Shankill, you suspect they're
being kept for tourists; there are black cab tours and everything.
Belfast's equivalent to the *City of God* tours of Brazilian favelas,
or an open-topped bus round the ruins of Detroit: the exploitation and, hopefully, neutralization of former sources of conflict
and humiliation. On closer investigation it's obvious that the
notion that these are mere remnants for show is no more true of
sectarianism than it's true of shanty towns or industrial decline.
This stuff is not a joke.

The Shankill, like most working-class areas of Belfast, was
redeveloped from the 1980s onwards in a manner which illu-
minates the roots of what is usually called 'defensible space'
planning. There are tiny, neo-Victorian houses in looping, intricate cul-de-sacs, providing vague, hostile, car-centred pedestrian
spaces and a grim visual straggliness. Their many blank gable ends
leave plenty of room for Oliver Cromwell, William of Orange,
the Ulster Volunteer Force and the Ulster Defence Association.
These kinds of paintings have been reclassified lately as 'folk art',
which no doubt they are, in the sense in which Communist com-
poser Hanns Eisler distinguished between reactionary 'folk' songs
and revolutionary 'mass' songs. The glasses, moustaches and tur-
tlenecks of the 1980s are immortalized in the portraits of various
gunwielders, but these murals know they're being looked at and
consumed. Some of them have notes on them, explaining otherwise esoteric symbolism such as the Red Hand of Ulster. One
less inflammatory mural features the apposite words, 'whatever

is about us not with us is not for us'. Windswept, unclaimed open space runs between the artworks. There's a lot of graffiti as well as the murals, but of an unusual sort. Most of it isn't even tags, but people scrawling their initials, so often and so densely that it looks like many of the streets have been randomly scribbled over. The houses are relatively new, but they look bitterly poor. A dour, brown-brick leisure centre tries to keep the kids busy, and on the Shankill Road itself, Union Jack bunting flutters in the wind. How can somewhere so evidently screwed over by successive governments of the United Kingdom find itself able to be *proud* of it?

The Interface Zone between the Shankill and Falls is fairly permeable. A fence running alongside a large flour mill is not so unusual; I later found that the fence is closed at night, but when it's open you might not bat an eyelid, but for the accompanying symbolism. The two areas are divided by an industrial estate put there for that very purpose. One of the sheds is now a church, which has the slogan 'Being a God-Influence'. Opposite, a mural welcomes you to the Shankill Road, if you're going in the opposite direction. 'We are *defiant, proud, welcoming*'. The welcome is a little lessened by the fact that the hither-gesturing hand on the painting is red. Then, past the fence, and you're in the Falls Road. There's one major difference, in that the murals are more right-on, so despite being English, being a Socialist I feel considerably less ill at ease. The Battle of the Boyne is replaced with a protest mural against the occupation of Palestine and a commemoration of the Nakba; Palestinian flags rather than Union Jacks (or more interestingly, the Tricolour) fly from the street. Hunger strikers and Republican taxi services aside, on the Falls murals Frederick Douglass replaces King Billy; Che Guevara appears instead of Cromwell.

Imagery is imagery, but in terms of architecture and planning, the Falls area shows absolutely identical defensible-space urbanism to the Shankill. Tiny semis and terraces around closes, with easily sealed-off entry and exit points, with grim 'public realm'. There are minor differences – the houses are in red brick rather than grey pebble-dash, and mercifully there are two points of architectural punctuation. The twin towers of St Peter's Cathedral, in the gaunt and spindly Celtic Gothic you can find at St Finbarr's in Cork, rise impressively over the Defensible hutches. Slightly further along the Falls Road, there's a good new leisure centre to keep the kids off the streets, a design by local architects Kennedy Fitzgerald in a brightly coloured but cliché-free modernist manner, looking positively optimistic in the circumstances. And there is a tower block: the Divis Tower, not exactly an imaginative design but recently renovated and decent-looking. Information panels remind you that it originally formed part of a dense, hard to police mid-rise deck-access complex, the Divis Flats, which was demolished and replaced with the houses you see today. The Divis Tower might just have been retained because it had, until recently, a British Army observation post on the roof.

As the most famous sectarian divide in Belfast, the Shankill-Falls model of urbanism could be considered something specific to Belfast, a form that emerged purely because of the need to stop people's houses being burnt down and car bombs from getting into housing estates. The late Martin Pawley listed the innovative features in a 1997 essay on architecture under the influence of terrorism: 'No new housing estate can be easily entered in a vehicle by one route and left by another. Except in a few old residential areas and where street patterns render it impossible, no car park or access road can be found within 12 metres of a residential building.'[19] Similarly, the open plans of streets, hard to police and easy to riot, were made into something controllable and enclosed. And yet it's hard to see this as remotely specific to Belfast (or Derry, or Portadown). In Liverpool in the 1980s a Trotskyist council replaced towers and tenements with a strikingly similar pattern of brick cul-de-sacs separated by perimeter walls; the suggestions of the ur-postmodernist Essex Design Guide in the mid-1970s enshrined the notion of 'Defensible Space' in speculative and public housing. Barratt Homes are planned in a not dissimilar way. And in the UK, rather than submitting plans to the army, we submit them to the police, in the form of Secured by Design, a legal requirement for any new area of social housing. The guidelines are almost exactly the same. What a visit to West Belfast does is make crystal clear the military roots of contemporary urban planning.

Lyrical South Belfast

There are parts of Belfast that weren't completely redesigned into encampments. Much of South Belfast, in the vicinity of the University, is distinctly more normal. After walking back to the centre, you walk in a straight line past, first of all, the Markets, a working-class area which lacks aggressively territorial murals, but which is planned in exactly the same 'defensible' manner as Shankill and Falls. The neo-Victorian architecture here is a little stronger, with nicely patterned brickwork, but the urbanism is identical, and perhaps worse, because the cordon sanitaire is less harsh – you're much closer to the centre, and it meets the grid via a pallid loop of terraces with a grass verge in front. Walk along the main road rather than through the maze of the Markets, and the break is not nearly so sharp. There are some decent industrial buildings, and a convincing, Brutalist-ish mill conversion at Somerset & Co, now Somerset Studios, where harsh concrete and red brick is reconfigured as chic rather than ignored altogether. There's also plenty of very luxurious and blingy-looking restaurants, something which makes it feel even more like Birmingham. Terraces both Regency and Victorian file off from here, and they don't appear to be divided by walls, bunting, murals or conspicuous swathes of wasteland.

Queen's University itself is a red-brick complex comparable to the University of Newcastle or other northern English colleges, a Victorian-Tudor style with some good modernist additions. On the other side is the Infirmary, a clad and tamed '70s futurist tower now dressed in white and gold. The real architectural interest lies further south, at the Botanic Gardens. Here, next to each other, are two buildings that are as original as anything anywhere in the UK or Eire, or elsewhere – two that guarantee Belfast's place in the most recondite of architectural history books. In the gardens itself is a Palm House by Richard Turner, who would later go on to design a much larger and more famous version in Kew, before the credit was swiped by Decimus Burton. This is not quite as freakish and epic, but it shows that the leap into ferro-vitreous dreamland in the 1840s was not entirely a matter of the imperial centre; it means that even modernist architecture, as much as modernist literature, may unexpectedly have to trace itself to Ireland. It's a bulbous, organic structure, crowded and rusty inside, and very appropriate to the prodigiously grey and rainy climate, a fantastical tropical insect set down in a darkened corner.

Francis Pym's mid-1960s extension to the Ulster Museum is just opposite. The existing Museum, begun in 1929 and left half-finished, was in a similar Edwardian baroque manner to the City Hall; it suggests that inter-war Ulster was as backwards as England with respect to twentieth-century architecture, a pallid, mechanistic and bland form of imperial classicism. Pym's extension is an act of aggression, there's absolutely no doubt about that – the façade is continued in Suprematist forms that owe more to the *Arkhitektons* of Kasimir Malevich than to any then-existing architecture. The coursing of the unfinished building is first continued in the extension, then suddenly broken up with a series of concrete geometries, wrapping around the side, where they form a fragmented, montaged façade; a Corbusian bull-horn profile runs along the bottom, to offer shelter and entrance. The extension keeps to the unfinished building's scale and classical symmetry, while making its protest very apparent. Under the curved concrete entrance is a café in green glass, the result of a recent refurbishment that caused apoplexy in local architects, mortified at the identikit pseudomodernism employed for a building as unique as this. As an urban object, in its parkland setting, it is still extremely powerful.

In the residential streets towards the river, Belfast's quirks mean that what looks like a very normal working-class Victorian area of industrial terraces turns out (when I mention it to anyone who lives in the city) to be the most affluent, middle-class district of the city. For whatever reason, there isn't a trace of sectarian imagery to be found. What you will find, just at the end of one entirely ordinary Victorian street, is O'Donnell and Tuomey's recently completed Lyric Theatre. This is well-made contextual modernism, in the 'other tradition' of modernist humanism that extends from Alvar Aalto to the British Library – the kind of building that makes architecture critics go dewy-eyed, muttering how they don't make them like that any more. There's no doubt that it approaches its site – a corner at the end of a descending row of terraces, opposite the Lagan – with great intelligence. The architects negotiate the slope, the gradation from the houses to the presence needed in a civic building, and the deep red of the materials with skill, wit and architectonic imagination, providing a series of different and complementary views depending on where the building is seen: the total opposite to the one-liners of Regeneration. For building in a residential and historically coherent area without resorting to the pieties of the vernacular and the 'reference', it is a textbook case of how to design well. Hence the applause. I have two caveats, though, one petty, one not. The latter concerns the florescence all the way down the sheer brick façade, an easily avoidable defect that makes it look considerably less old-school in its constructional expertise. The former is the absurdly overpriced café. Regardless – all three of these buildings are worth an architectural pilgrimage in themselves, although the notion that architectural visits could help the city in some way is hard to credit. Especially so on the other side of the river, in East Belfast.

'It was fine when it left us'

I thought it would be interesting and informative to see if it was possible to walk from the residential working-class areas of East Belfast to the new 'Titanic Quarter' adjacent. It is – but I felt lucky to be alive at the end of it. Not because of the sectariana, alarming as that is, but for more prosaic reasons. At first, the route I took from Laganside across the river was, again, only particularly depressing if you've not visited similar schemes in Birmingham, Leeds or elsewhere; normality, again, of a sort. Nobody in the UK would bat an eyelid at the apartment blocks, with their warehouse 'references' and warehouse joylessness; nor at the Thames Valley-like retail-park style of a banks' and outsourcers' HQ, the Lesley Exchange, with its glass stair towers and 'stone' cladding. Only the still very fortified-looking Central Railway Station suggests anything aberrant. The streets are Victorian, though the very wide arterial roads are not. In the distance are a pair of structures that are striking in their gigantism – the monumental cranes of Harland and Wolff, shipbuilders, who still carry on a small modicum of trade nearby. The cranes have names – Samson and Goliath. Harland and Wolff were, of course, the builders of the Titanic. I grew up in the port from which the Titanic sailed, a city which now has an only slightly smaller population than Belfast, although Belfast's metropolitan ambitions are as clear in Samson and Goliath as in Donegall Square. You'll have seen these cranes already if you've approached Belfast from the north, or from the sea – gaunt Sant'Elian archways that frame views of the city from the Westlink. They were installed in the '70s as a gesture of confidence in the industrial city, Troubles or no Troubles. That their function is presently vestigial is hardly evidence for the uniqueness of Belfast's problems. Tall, held up on alternately thin and bulkily angular supports, with mini-cranes on each side, they embody the sort of industry the Italian futurists fantasized about. They appear on postcards for sale at the airport.

The street signs round here are bilingual, Gaelic and English. The area is Short Strand, a tiny nationalist enclave in loyalist territory. Its urban form is more irregular than in the two rival defensible spaces of Shankill and Falls, as much larger Victorian fragments survive, albeit with the streetline around them completely reconfigured. A long row of terraces is next to a huge cleared site, on which Housing Associations plan to build. Some of these red-brick terraces could easily be in Middlesbrough; others have doorways that look almost Georgian. In amongst them are several closes and cul-de-sacs placed as enclosure, breakers-up of the grid; bungalows and even a bit of quasi-modernist Aalto-esque infill. The murals are, in some cases, pretty mild – Sinn Fein electoral campaigns, people learning Gaelic, kids playing in the Victorian terraces with the cranes in the background. The mural to INLA hunger striker Mickey Devine, surmounted by a red flag dedicated to the small, ultra-violent, far-left Republican organization is as heated as it gets. After that, you pass through the Peace Line. A tiny space lined with walls, that could easily have (and probably at times had) a turnstile, and, once again, the houses are the same and the murals are completely different.

Again, 1980s–90s cul-de-sacs interspersed with small nine-teenth-century workers' barracks, again very obvious poverty;

the only unlikeness is in the presence of Union Jack and red-hand bunting, or the content of the gable-end murals. The latter are, here, utterly schizophrenic. There's the Titanic, 'ship of dreams' on one wall; on another, 'NO MORE', and two children shaking hands over a graveyard, with a poem underneath celebrating the end of the violence. Another is being painted as I walk past. It's almost monochrome, showing a funeral procession guarded by two balaclava'd men with machine guns in the foreground. Each of the marching figures wears dark glasses and a face mask. Later, on my way back to the centre, I see more in this stark, monochrome, violent style, presumably by the same artist – commissioned, I'm told, by the local commander for the Ulster Volunteer Force, who is alleged to have been behind a full-scale riot here a few months ago in June 2011, in which shots were fired at police; somewhat overshadowed by the riots across the Irish Sea two months later. I also see a Peace Line more pointedly defensive than any others – it's a rampart, brick blast walls with metal fences above, taller than any of the houses than run alongside it. The houses near the Interface have permanent metal grilles over their windows, as I noticed coming back from the Titanic Quarter.

Northern Ireland, which for pretty obvious reasons has a large public sector, is one of David Cameron's targets for 'shrinking the state'; one of the allegedly babied areas that must be weaned. Those youths who were fighting in Short Strand were largely unemployed, and there will be a lot more of them soon. That's

not to suggest that there has not been private-sector investment; its flagship is that aforementioned Quarter, which takes up a chunk of the Harland and Wolff site. To get there from residential East Belfast, you have to traverse a swathe of motorway without any pedestrian crossings, and here is where walking feels a little like taking your life in your hands. Someone has obviously walked it before you, though, as there's a small piece of graffiti on the concrete of the bridge, in small handwriting so you have to look closely: 'Only the English understand cruelty. Cunt.' There is literally no other way to the place on foot; the route from here to there is about as friendly to the walker as the route from Bluewater to Ebbsfleet International. This is apt enough, as the planner and architect for the Quarter is Bluewater's creator-of-community, Eric Kuhne.

The neighbour here is not a disused quarry or a container port but a residential, working-class area, and one that might well be in some straits. It would have been nice to try and make some attempt to connect the Quarter to East Belfast. Enterprise Zones are not made of such things, and in fairness Belfast City Council would have had to demolish part of the motorway to do so. It is instead, in an act of pure folly, being extended. When you finally reach it, the roads and the mild-modernist offices and hotels that loop around them are planned as an arc, which must have made a pretty pattern on the drawing board. The 'public' part entails an architecturally inoffensive college and the Odyssey Arena, a gross, lumbering, introverted troll of a building. It gets really exciting, though, when you make it to the point where the Titanic Quarter meets the remains of the shipyards. A shattered ticket booth for a car park, an acre or so of rubble, the cranes in sublime proximity across the sheds, and a sandstone office block very like the one in Barrow. Behind it, waving its arms in the air so you notice it, is the Titanic Visitor Centre, which is the Icon; it takes the sharp, exploded forms and metallic surfaces of an old Danny Libeskind building, the sort that was supposed to symbolize conflict and disjunction, and gives it beaux-arts symmetry, which may not have been the original idea. The symbolism here is not at all ambiguous. It's an iceberg. Do you see? The official slogan for this apocalypse, found on the advertisements, is:

'The Titanic Quarter. We used to make ships here — now we make communities.'

The Demarcation Breaks Up

It would be hugely unfair to give the impression that all of this is going unchallenged. In fact, there's a degree of ideas and resistance here which the cities that Belfast resembles would be lucky to have. For instance, the Forum for Alternative Belfast have published a plan for building on the surface car parks and wastes around the ring road, in order not merely to eliminate the subtopian slurry that surrounds the grid, but to establish some tangible coherence to the city, to give the rest of it the easy link between centre and residential area that only South Belfast has at present. It's the sort of idea that has hardly helped make Manchester a more equal city, and it may be easily criticized as Richard Rogers-issue sermonizing on the virtues of dense and compact cities; but Belfast obviously needs this sort of intervention more than most places. A simple visual and spatial link between West Belfast and the centre wouldn't solve its problems, but would surely make a positive difference; even more a real link between the Titanic Quarter and Short Strand. Architect Mark Hackett of the Forum drove me around North Belfast at the end of my visit. It was the only part of the journey conducted by car, and that became something I was very pleased about. Here, past Crumlin Road and leading on to Ardoyne, the relatively simple demarcation of Shankill and Falls is replaced by an illegible chaos of peace lines, both new and long-lasting. So, it's hard to tell the difference between outer Birmingham and outer Walsall — well, here that difficulty has been militarized.

Belfast was not part of Pathfinder, the New Labour scheme to demolish working-class housing and replace it with something more aspirational; but in North Belfast you could be forgiven for thinking it had. Once more, the Northern Irish capital appears to be doing much the same thing with its cities as England, only for what are on the face of it different reasons. Here, sometimes nondescript and sometimes handsome Victorian housing is left derelict and then demolished when tensions along an Interface

Zone start to run too high; in the process, large swathes of the northern suburbs look like they've just faced a random V-2 attack. Next to one of these dereliction interfaces is a park, with a Berlin Wall through it to stop the youth from starting riots. Nearby, adjoining a relatively decent housing development, where there are at least vague hints of streets rather than cul-de-sacs and a convincing re-use of local red brick, is Belfast's only privately-funded peace line. It was a condition of the development, because it was assumed that demographic changes meant that members of one of the 'communities' would be more likely to be living in the new development than members of the other, who had hitherto lived in that area. So their semi-detached houses have running behind them a white-painted concrete wall. In another of the battered interface areas a spit of scrubland has some shipping containers on it, on which Sina's convenience store sells its wares. It's a long way from East London's outposts of Container Chic like Boxpark or Trinity Buoy Wharf. The shop serves both groups, with seats outside and a café inside. It seems to work. In their wisdom, Belfast council have refused to grant the container and its owner permission to use the site. It seems an unlikely place for a 'stunning development', but hope springs eternal.

Sometimes all this has positive architectural outcomes. Castellated linen mills tower over an '80s council house noddy-land; industrial estates crop up at random points, making the perimeter walls look less obvious. At the entrance back into the city centre, past the derelict Crumlin Road courthouse, slated to become flats but derelict for years (Barry Gilligan has to answer for this, too), past a heavy Victorian jail (the one which internment filled so full that the H-Blocks were built), past an Orange Hall which, apparently, recently removed its protective metal screen (reasons to be cheerful!), you find two magnificently aggressive, exuberant and soaring Victorian churches facing off against each other, the sectarian animus proving a great spur to wilfully taste-less architectural imagination. It is however a macabre pleasure, and so is Belfast urbanism in general. Here is a city riven with divisions, whose post-Troubles redevelopment has somehow *multiplied* walls both real and perceived. It's incredibly disturb-ing, I repeat, not for its difference from the rest of the UK, but its similarity. All the factors – rampant inequality, deindustriali-zation, social divisions and poverty – are as familiar as the city centre's buildings. Sectarianism might be mere torchpaper, or a particularly violent distraction from the obvious. With unem-ployment about to explode, what will happen here in the next few years? When Belfast is weaned off the state, will the young men of East Belfast all get jobs in the Titanic Quarter's Premier Inn, or will they not? These questions notwithstanding, for the rest of the country, contemporary Belfast could so easily be a vision of the future. Peace lines in Clapham are not implausible.

Forum aside, there is one major cause for optimism in Belfast's built environment. The area around Victoria Square may be booming of a Saturday afternoon, but the northern peripheries of the city centre get squalid quick; at one intersection, you have a street leading off towards the Shankill that is mostly boarded up, which in the case of the shop selling weaponry may have been a good thing. A lot of former commercial buildings here are der-elict, either because they're being sat upon by developers waiting for the recovery, or in many cases because the sites are owned by NAMA, the 'bad bank' that handles the Republic of Ireland's assets. They may all of course end up as loft living solutions,

but given the unlikeliness of that recovery, a major question is begged. And a particularly urgent answer is given in the Bank of Ireland building. This is in an area that could perhaps have been marketed as Belfast's Deco Quarter, should that have had a sufficiently historic resonance. Ornate inter-war moderne buildings with strongly expressed corner façades face each other; the best of them is this Portland stone bank, its Mini-Manhattan clock tower now with a banner across it reading 'OCCUPY BELFAST'. The wings to the street feature the slogan 'IT'S NOT A RECESSION, IT'S A ROBBERY'. On my second visit, in January 2012, the occupiers had just turned up here, moving in from their campsite in front of Ulster University; it seemed a much smarter choice, and not just for the shelter. They were still debating what to do with the space – inside, their sleeping bags were within the tents. A homeless shelter, a social centre, a space in the heart of the city where they could hurl their defiance at it. One of the occupiers tells me: 'Oh, we know about all the disused buildings in Belfast. We're going to take them, one by one.'

Chapter Eighteen

The City of London:
The Beginning is Nigh

Occupy versus New Urbanism

If you looked up above St Paul's Cathedral in the early afternoon of 9 November 2011, you could have counted at least three helicopters. Their deafening spiralling nearly drowned out what was happening below. There was a student protest, marching nearby in Moorgate, massively over-policed as revenge for past slips; it intended, though failed, to link up with an ongoing occupation outside St Paul's. All this made the 9th a perfect day to explore this neurotically protected citadel of undead financial capitalism. The City of London is the smallest and oldest place that is covered in this book: the Roman colonial city that became the English capital that became an eerily depopulated autonomous centre of gentlemanly finance. Once the incarnation in space of the British Empire's funding system, since 1986 it has taken on another life. Still not residential, still unencumbered by representative democracy or common law, the City has become the fulcrum of a system of offshore, unregulated finance, sprouting colonies on the Isle of Dogs, Borough, Holborn (which it has recently rebranded as 'Midtown'), Aldgate and Farringdon (if not Birmingham, Leeds and Edinburgh). It is Old Corruption in braced glass, the satanic site at the heart of the UK's malaise. Where shall we begin the indictment? Suburbanization, the evacuation of the city and the creation of single-class enclaves practically began here in the eighteenth century, when the coffee houses were replaced by Clubs and their habitués escaped westwards. Here, chaps made themselves fabulously rich on the proceeds of slavery and rapine. Here, in the late nineteenth and twentieth century, a form of capitalism fit for gentlemen, seemingly detached from the muck of industry, became so successful that it considered itself fit to dictate to the rest of the country. Here, our livelihoods are frittered away as part of a cocaine-fuelled casino; here, you are paid a bonus for creating a double-dip recession. Here, government policy is dictated. It sounds like demagoguery, but then the City's activities have long been so rapacious as to be almost parodic, a bad Soviet satirist's impression of capitalism. A serious reckoning is well overdue.

The occupiers had aimed to take the London Stock Exchange, but in the process they had settled on a prime architectural embodiment of their target. Encircling St Paul's, where the Church of England was morally embarrassed into giving the occupiers succour, is Paternoster Square. This was once the City's printers' quarter; here in 1940, when the bombs rained down on St Paul's, the hoses were pointed towards the Cathedral rather than its hinterland, leading to the near-total destruction of a piece of working urban fabric. The redevelopment as towers, low-rise offices and a public square so scandalized the Prince of Wales that his architectural tastes were fully catered for in the 1990s redevelopment,

masterplanned by William Whitfield. It's a simulacrum of what was there before, full of signifiers of 'London' but without much correspondence to anything that previously existed here. The main face to the street was Juxon House, a nasty, tacky Vegas via Mussolini's Italy via Duchy of Cornwall neoclassical superblock. In the last decade, the City has been at the forefront of the new pseudomodernism, so this development has always stuck out for its kitsch revanchism. It almost seems deliberate – the City letting the future king settle a score, so that it could scandalize him with each further development. Entering the 'public', privately owned and privately patrolled Paternoster Square, you walk under the gate of the early-eighteenth-century Temple Bar, attributed to Wren. It was dismantled by the Victorians and sold off for someone's garden in Enfield. And here it is again: a long way from the Temple, but fitting entirely with the paraphernalia all around, such as the ludicrous approximation of the Monument that towers at the heart of the square.

There was the ghost of a town planning idea in this collection of ostentatiously contextual banks and offices, in the way they enclosed the great dome with a series of narrow byways, attempting to replicate the City's medieval street plan. This has long been one of twenty-first-century London's most depressing, smugly jolly spaces. Not now, though. The silly mock-pathetic columns of Juxon House, each of them topped by a broken, blank-eyed Grecian head, were covered by the occupiers, making them an *architecture parlante* – hundreds of small posters, flyers, messages, notes, manifestos, declarations. 'GENERAL STRIKE!' reads the aptest, with a wild-eyed cat below. 'THE BEGINNING IS NIGH!' reads one, 'BEAUTY IS IN THE STREET' another, which is quite Urban Renaissance of them, though the poster's image of a barricade-laden thoroughfare is not very Urban Splash – and nor is the highly developed public infrastructure of the camp the graphic collage accompanies. In tents large and small are a University, Welfare centre, Clinic, Restaurant, Public Toilets (the latter especially unusual in contemporary London). The tents themselves are a Drop City of simple, curvilinear frames covered with multicoloured tensile artificial fabric – high-tech, though their users might not always think so. A line of armoured riot police, shields and truncheons at the ready, stand at the other side of Temple Bar, with the pastiche of the Monument in the background. As an example of *détournement*, a subverting of private space into public space, you really couldn't do better; it's a wonderful irony that the Yard's part-ownership by the Church has meant that the encampment is outside Paternoster Square, of all places (though there are subsidiary occupations at the time of writing – a 'Bank of Ideas' in a disused bank in Broadgate, and another tent encampment in the genuinely public, municipally-owned Finsbury Square). And, for months, they stayed here, a semi-permanent experiment in propaganda and direct democracy. It was the most exciting thing to happen to the City of London since the Lloyd's Building. Or the fire.

Enjoy Your Spectacle!

I have differences with the occupiers, and they are outlined to some degree at the end of this chapter. But what they have hit upon here, under the influence of Climate Camp, Occupy Wall Street and the student movement of 2010–11, is extremely smart: the move away from the notion of protest as a brief 'carnival' accompanying a ruling-class summit, or a march from A to B, and the attempt instead to become *un*-spectacular, to become a feature of the urban landscape. The experience of the protests outside of the Bank of England during the G20 meetings, in April 2009, an event billed as the 'G20 Meltdown', is relevant here. Due to a combination of cowardice, claustrophobia and Crohn's disease, I do not react well to being 'kettled' at marches – that increas-ingly popular police tactic which involves penning in a group of protesters, waiting until they get pissed off enough at being penned in that tempers fray and stuff starts getting thrown, then piling in with the shields, pepper spray and truncheons. I tend to moan, and/or panic. So the plan that day, at least as far as I was concerned, was to get as close to the protest as possible without getting kettled. In this I failed entirely, and was not allowed to leave for three hours. After several attempts to get through the police lines with my new shiny NUJ Press Pass (helpful police comments: 'Try the end of the police line', 'Dunno, I'm just calling my boss', 'Go up Bartholomew Lane', 'Try Lombard St', and best of all 'Try over there, but it depends who you ask'), I eventually made it – the friends I had abandoned emerged about fifteen minutes later, thanks to the reported 'breaking of a police line'. Those who didn't escape then were held until midnight. So, I'm not all that well disposed to the tactic where you reclaim the street by letting the police imprison you in it; but there's something at these marches you don't see at the more well-organized, well-stewarded ones, such as the decidedly plodding demonstration that preceded the G20 protests by a few days. The chants are more darkly funny, the costumes are better, there are fewer 'carnivalesque' samba bands, and placards such as 'Harm Bono' and 'You try for ages to destroy capitalism, and then it destroys itself' were a cut above the standard issue.

Nonetheless, the G20 protests, and the many 'carnivals against capitalism' that preceded them, were purely spectacularized affairs, something acknowledged by the protesters themselves ('Enjoy Your Spectacle!', read one graffito on the Royal Exchange), by the media (even before the RBS windows got smashed, professional photographers made up a goodly portion of us in the kettle) and by the police, who in a sense gave a proportion of the crowd exactly what they wanted. It showed the final uselessness as a concept and protesting tactic of the 'Temporary Autonomous Zone'. But before we bury it, we should acknowledge exactly why this was initially so persuasive a tactic, in both political and geographical terms. The City of London is a place ringed by steel even on the most mundane rainy Tuesday, and when filled with protesters, it presents a spectacle of the latent becoming suddenly blindingly obvious, as the quiet surveillance and police presence becomes thumpingly loud and brutal – something made especially apparent, when those unkettled had to give their names and submit to being photographed.

A protest in the City also creates curious juxtapositions of authoritarian architecture and the actual forces of authority. You could see a line of police in front of the Bank of England, Herbert Baker's horribly crass, clumsy 1930s edifice; a building parasitic upon John Soane's original (and, as an eighteenth-century anti-riot gesture, windowless) ground floor, a classicism that imitates the past while actively destroying it. The plod were lined up in front of the reduced-classical sculptures on the building's frontage, redolent of Hitler's favoured sculptor Arno Breker. Conversely, the Climate Camp protesting nearby in Bishopsgate were setting up something genuinely adaptable and indeterminate in the shadow of the Lloyd's building. There is an urbanist lesson in there also. The City should, in theory, have been an enormously difficult place to kettle, given the complexity of that medieval street plan, the diametric opposite of those Haussmannian anti-barricade boulevards. In response, every alley, passage, cross-street and underpass was blocked by lines of police. After being unkettled, I walked around streets of offices where you could see, readied, vehicles more usually employed in 1970s Northern Ireland, or groups of riot police psyching themselves up like American footballers. The security landscape became blindingly, barbarically obvious. This should in theory have contrasted with the area within the protest itself, with its own transformation of space, but whether this was noticed by the office workers of this already deeply enclosed and protected area of London is a decidedly moot point. So who was this demonstration *for*?

The zone created was certainly temporary, but in no sense whatever was it autonomous, as the entire area was sealed off with remarkably little difficulty, and the potential – which, by being broadcast to those outside of the 5,000 inside the kettle, was necessarily a spectacle – of a reclaimed space, an area of work and capital turned over to the ludic, was easily replaced with a spectacle of boredom, violence and aimless inertia. Worst of all, a spectacle of ritual. A tactic of this sort could only work on a far wider scale, where a large area – which could become part of everyday life, not be contained within a fixed boundary – were reclaimed. That would be a question of numbers as much as of tactics. The Climate Camp had a linked, but dissimilar problem. Obviously determined *not* to give the *Evening Standard* what it wanted, they reacted to the riot police's attempt to sweep them off Bishopsgate by putting their hands in the air and chanting 'This is not a riot' – only to face almost exactly the same treatment. Except that their (televised) spectacle became in the process far more effective. It's no surprise, then, that the Occupy movement, or UK Uncut, have effectively picked up the slack after the farcical end to the 'G20 Meltdown'.

Groundscrapers and Stealth Buildings

Given that some of the experience I've described is garnered from protesting in rather than walking through the City, the malevolence of the place is taken as given in this chapter. It is also, which should be somewhat shaming, perhaps the most coherently planned UK city of the last twenty years. This is something of a negative virtue. Compared with the planning of the inner areas of Birmingham, Edinburgh, Glasgow, Manchester, Bristol, the tenure of City Planning Officer Peter Rees since 1985 can be seen as a relatively benevolent despotism; the nearest UK equivalent to the expensive stone-clad faux-austerity of, say, contemporary Berlin, although much more picturesque and irregular. You can see it at its most impressive at night, on a train passing into Cannon Street, where a riverside crammed with decorous glazed ziggurats with skyscrapers and St Paul's behind them provides one of the twenty-first-century British city's few analogues to the

cities of the future we'd all grown up on in science fiction. On the ground, in the daytime, new City buildings boast expensive materials, fine detailing, and sometimes a degree of cleverness in their adaptation to the old City's streets, courtyards and alleyways, to which they are mostly forced, to some degree, to conform. Sometimes the resultant urban picturesque is purely accidental, as when skyscrapers poke out from the edges of a curved passage; elsewhere, it has become a virtue. The architects are seldom the grunts, the commercial architects who churn out much of what actually gets built in Urban Britain – Broadway Malyan, Benoy, Hamiltons, Chapman Taylor, Capita, BDP, Aedas – but talented if often bloodless starchitects like Eric Parry, Richard Rogers, Jean Nouvel, or blue-chip multinationals such as Skidmore Owings Merrill or Kohn Pedersen Fox. It's not a recipe for joy, flights of fancy or imagination, but it shows a degree of architectural decency that contrasts amusingly with the nihilism which pays for them.

There's roughly one success to one howler, all built around the same time; the most interesting schemes, if we suspend non-architectural judgement, are those which pay most attention to the unique montage of the City's built fabric. The area around Wood Street has particularly good going. Richard Rogers' twin towers are perhaps his finest post-Lloyd's works in the capital, an asymmetrical glazed Gothic; nearby is a mid-rise office block by Eric Parry that is elegantly and expensively authoritarian, evidently inspired by the Mussolini style of McMorran & Whitby's Wood Street Police Station, a very late (post-war) classical tower with podium. 'Radical' architecture is represented by the Office for Metropolitan Architecture's new building for Rothschilds. This is exaggeratedly site-specific; it is crammed into a tiny spot next to Wren's St Stephen Walbrook, a building which is itself a compendium of all the different architectural devices that can be crammed into a very small space. Close up, Rothschild's is clumsy and irritating, with its irregular steel mullions in vague reference to the World Trade Centre; from the other side of the river its fiddliness suddenly makes sense, as you see how it rises into a glazed boardroom on stilts, a surreal image of contemporary plutocracy.

There are dozens, also, of new office blocks that you can't tell are new office blocks – façade jobs, where drab but 'historic' bankers' classical is riveted onto steel-framed, open-plan offices. Then there are the 'groundscrapers', the long, low office blocks which couldn't go higher because they'd interfere with the views of St Paul's. The best of these are those which embrace the basically sinister, shadowy, unregulated nature of the City's activities – the black glass and spiky steel mullions of KPF's extension to the old *Daily Express* building, or, nearby, Peter Foggo's Gotham construction in blue stone. It stands adjacent to James Stirling's Number One Poultry, which in that context is like a Brooks Bros suit accessorized with comedy neckwear from Tie Rack, a screamingly City-Boy building, aggressive and bumptious, an overbearing pub bore. There are currently attempts afoot to rehabilitate buildings like this from their former critical obloquy, and while it's possible to admire Stirling's spatial mastery and density of architectural expression, it's also impossible to contemplate such noxious jollity without feeling slightly ill. Mies van der Rohe designed a tower for this site. After a protracted fight between conservationists and developers, Number One Poultry is what occurred. It's certainly more apt. The other 'groundscrapers' don't even have the overbearing wit of Poultry – typical is Foster's Walbrook Building, a crouching armadillo in banded steel. A more unusual effort is the attempt to bring non-banking activities into the City at Jean Nouvel's One New Change, a confused, desolate and cold space. All this said, even the bad buildings here have a sensitivity of massing and materials that is deeply unusual in Britain. The Devil doesn't necessarily have the best buildings, but he can afford slightly more civilized ones. Don't think too hard about what goes on inside and there's often something to grudgingly admire. There's another kind of City building, though; one which practically forces you to have an opinion on it.

Skyscrapers for Bus Stops

The suggestion here that City planning takes its context seriously might sound counter-intuitive, given its obvious vertical emphasis of late. The architectural results show American corporate modernism made more interesting by being slotted at random into the street's non-plan, creating strongly memorable accidental vistas. The Gherkin still feels like a piece of CGI up close, and SOM's Broadgate Tower is squat where it should be soaring, but KPF's Heron Tower is more impressive – sleek from the south side, its heavy-engineering backside is presented to hip, faux-industrial Shoreditch. The Heron is, at the time of writing, largely empty. All are the ultimate result of Ken Livingstone's failed Faustian Pact in the early 2000s – skyscrapers for Section 106 agreements, and a manifestly misguided attempt by a Greater London Authority without tax-raising powers to finance infrastructural improvements and new social housing, resulting in a few 'affordable' studio flats slotted behind waterside yuppie-dromes. Seen from, say, the viewing area of Tate Modern, the new City skyscrapers compare well with Canary Wharf's axial beaux-arts boredom, appearing genuinely distinctive and peculiar, a montage skyline. Those towers that have been built, and even some of those unbuilt, are now 'iconic' – taken, apparently, to Londoners' hearts in a way that is rare for London's tall buildings. This is a very surprising development. Centre Point most famously, but also the NatWest Tower and the '70s cluster around it, were for decades ciphers for architectural boredom and malevolence. In that, they're not untypical; La Défense or Frankfurt are held in similarly low esteem.

In *The Sphere and the Labyrinth*, the architectural historian Manfredo Tafuri claimed that 'no better way exists of grasping what the American skyscraper is *not* than by studying how European culture has attempted to assimilate and translate it into its own terms.' For him, the problem here was a fundamental point-missing; Europeans were convinced, erroneously, that the skyscraper was 'architecture'. On the contrary, wrote Tafuri, they were 'real live bombs with chain effects, designed to explode the entire real estate market'. They were an exemplar of capitalism at its limits, 'an instrument – and no longer an "expression" – of economic policy'. From the 1870s to the 1940s, the steel frames of these speculative megaliths were clad after construction in historicist ornament, but that too was driven by economic motives

– designed purely to reassure, to give an impression of solidity. The freakish, irrational shapes of American capitalism was translated across the Atlantic into 'high architecture', and in the process the original delirium was lost; an explanation, perhaps, for the libidinal deficiencies of Birmingham or Croydon's central 'mini-Manhattans'.

London's experience with tall buildings is more riven with controversies and high-profile failures than anywhere else. Yet the City is now starting to complete one of the most dramatic and gestural new skylines anywhere in the world, topped, inescapably, just outside of its borders, by Renzo Piano's 'Shard'. How did this happen? In Britain's brief burst of post-war social democracy, tall buildings were not skyscrapers but high-rises, serving useful purposes – they were housing, largely, freeing up green space in the new council estates. Because of this, the better tall buildings are nearly all residential, educational or in some way connected with the Welfare State; it wasn't until the late 1960s that the capital's financial district even began to build what would once have been called skyscrapers. This was partly the result of the old City's refusal to accommodate modernism, its suspicion, pre-Big Bang, of anything outside of its own traditions. By the early '60s its new buildings and bombsite replacements were still generally neoclassical or otherwise non-modernist. The results were mainly deadly, Portland stone edifices that Plymouth would have rejected as too stodgy; though there are some wilfully odd exceptions, such as the aforementioned Wood Street Police Station or Bracken House, Albert Richardson's sandstone, Chicago School edifice opposite St Paul's: an office block for the *Financial Times*, its ornamented doorway features a depiction of Winston Churchill as a Sun God, which says a great deal about the aesthetics of the post-war City. So when it did 'go modernist' at the end of that decade, it did so reluctantly.

Aside from a few minor essays in Mies van der Rohe imitation by the firm Gollins Melvin Ward, the most visible of these early skyscrapers were the dozen or so designed by the corporate architect Colonel Richard Seifert, in a style initially indebted to the sleek, chic Milan work of Gio Ponti, or the sensual, patterned modernism of Oscar Niemeyer – the demolished London

Bridge Tower exemplified the former, Centre Point in the West End the latter. Subsequently Seifert developed a more original, sombre, sinister, paranoid manner exemplified by the inscrutable NatWest Tower, until the early 2000s the City's tallest building. Interestingly, Seifert has been all but forgotten. There is no monograph on his work, at least three of his London towers have been demolished, and only one, Centre Point, is listed. Yet their dominance of the skyline continues, rivalled only by Christopher Wren, and more recently, Norman Foster. And then came the new generation known as 'Ken's Towers', and a neophyte embrace of glass and steel by stock-brick and concrete London.

Skyscrapers' close link with capitalist crisis is legendary. The famous 'skyscraper index' entails plotting financial crashes (1929, 1974, 1997, 2008) against the completion of successive 'world's tallest' towers (Empire State Building, World Trade Centre, Petronas Towers, Burj Khalifa). London, again, conforms to type – Centre Point was most famous for lying empty and unlet, in a city with endemic homelessness; in the 1970s, London's 'Architects' Revolutionary Council' proclaimed that 'we wish to create a situation whereby every time a student passes a building such as Centre Point he vows that he will never work in a practice that is involved in such obscenities'. When the derivatives and property-based boom of the Blair era led to a massive demand for office space, the City and its Docklands outpost were forced once again to build upwards – yet the example of the 1960s had unpleasant associations. One Canada Square indicated this could be done, though it had never been particularly popular. Then Ken Livingstone, elected as a left-wing protest candidate but very quickly ingratiating himself with the City of London, became convinced of the need for a new skyline – partly due to the aforementioned Faustian Pact, and partly, it seems, after being dazzled by a visit to Shanghai. And so the appropriate planning restrictions were lifted.

A tower designed by Norman Foster showed the way forward. Officially, Foster's skyscraper on the site of the IRA-bombed Baltic Exchange was first called the 'Swiss Re tower' after its sponsors, and after they sold it, '30 St Mary Axe', after its address; but it will always be 'the Gherkin' to most. Calculated or

not, the nicknaming was a masterstroke – the Cockney homeliness and domesticity of the name suggested that the alien object had earned some kind of public affection. This was something no previous London tower had achieved; and its unironically phallic nature may have helped (it features as a psychoanalyst's office in the hilarious London-based *Basic Instinct 2*). After the Gherkin, a whole raft of towers was announced, almost simultaneously, and all of them were given cutesy domestic nicknames. The Walkie-Talkie. The Cheesegrater. The Helter-Skelter. Tallest of all is the Shard, outside of the City's jurisdiction but very much part of this story. The Shard is the only one of these towers to have pre-emptively used a possible nickname as its actual, 'official' name, and a board with 'SHARD' emblazoned upon it has been London's tallest object for some months at the time of writing.

Intended to be the tallest building in Europe, it was soon overtaken by Moscow's City of Capitals, but its striking disjunction with its surroundings indicates something rather unprecedented. This is London's first 'supertall' skyscraper, putting it in the exalted company of the Sears Tower, the Shanghai World Financial Centre, the Petronas Towers, and Dubai's notorious Burj; and it really is one of Tafuri's 'real live bombs'. Its base is so enormous that two earlier high-rises, one by Seifert, were

demolished to make way for it. From a distance, as intended, it is
one sheer work, delicate and coherent; on the ground, it's a mess,
with mini-towers the size of a tall council block bolted onto it at
the corners, as if it wasn't bulky enough. The effect on Borough,
the area into which it has crashed, is truly disastrous. The terraces
and tenements around are not so much dwarfed as bullied into
silence, subject to an act of urban thuggery. Meanwhile, around
London Bridge station an extraordinary network of ad hoc walkways leads the pedestrian on a jagged route to traverse the site.
On the south bank of the Thames, the Shard has no 'cluster'
as company, or to soften the blow. It is deforming to the urban
fabric, explosive in its context, and yet, in its unfinished form,
thrilling to behold.

The somewhat sickening thrill has been in watching the Shard
go up, watching a tiny skeleton staff of builders erect this gigantic
glass edifice, with its bowels still on display; watching it imprint
upon the London skyline the rude stub of its concrete lift core,
watching the bare steel frame stack up as glass panels chase close
behind. Just as in the Gothic skyscrapers of 1900s Chicago, in the
completed work all of this is effaced in order to create an entirely
seamless effect, a pure and ethereal 'shard of glass' without any
trace of human hands – but certainly intended to evoke the pen
of its architect, Renzo Piano. Anyone keen that architects observe
some kind of urban order, some sense of scale, some dignity or
rectitude in the London townscape, would be mortified by the
sheer aggression and arrogance of the Shard. It would be advis-
able for them to journey west to the City's borders – the area of
Holborn recently rebranded as 'Midtown' – to Central St Giles,
next to Centre Point, where another tower by Renzo Piano was
planned. After heritage objections finished that off, this expensive
mixed-use scheme had suddenly to shrink down, while still main-
taining the requisite level of profit on the investment. The result
is an atrocious botch-job, a bunch of extremely dense, stocky and
inelegant blocks crammed into the site, with a grim postage stamp
of public space in the middle; in order to distract attention from
this act of violence, Piano decided to colour the entire thing in
lurid yellows, oranges and greens. It's an embarrassing building,
with none of the confidence and clarity of the Shard – and if there

is an alternative, serving the same functions, then the Shard is what it looks like. If one accepts the system that produces these buildings, one has also to accept that they will be tall, very tall.

The Shard is, more than absolutely anything else in the UK, a definitive glass gravestone for the 1990s and 2000s' tentative, half-hearted attempts at urban and architectural reform under the direction of Piano's former partner, Richard Rogers. The Urban Task Force that he led, and the planning advice he gave to Ken Livingstone, entailed making neoliberalism *look* nicer. There would be speculative blocks of flats, but a Commission for Architecture and the Built Environment would assess them, and sometimes give their developers a stern telling-off. There would be giant office blocks, but they would be designed by first-rank, blue-chip international architects like Rafael Vinoly or Renzo Piano (when the Shard was first mooted under John Major, the architects were to be local hacks Broadway Malyan). The results are only now coming to completion under an anti-urban, Conservative government and Mayoralty, and it's hard, looking at the chaos around the Shard, or the extreme inequalities it incarnates, to imagine this was what Rogers or Livingstone originally had in mind. Next to the Shard is another high-rise, once the tallest in London south of the Thames, now a mere pipsqueak – the Brutalist 1970s tower of Guy's Hospital, an especially extraordinary survival given that inner-urban hospitals have been pressured to sell their lucrative land and move to peripheral locations, as part of the Private Finance Initiative. It will soon be reclad, to be 'in keeping' with the Shard.

The Shard, largely owned by the property investment fund Qatari Diar, is intended to house high-end offices, luxury flats, a hotel and a spa. The notion that London could erect a block of council housing or an NHS hospital as one of the pivotal objects on its skyline is now unthinkable. And for that, the lame conformism of a generation that wanted to make neoliberal capitalism more rational and more elegant is chiefly responsible.

The Dining Room in the Oil Rig

It is, today, hard to ponder the architectural qualities or otherwise of the City; it's a recherché of perverse pleasure, like admiring the design of prisons. There's plenty of interest, but it's not the sort of thing you'd admit to in company. Especially when you consider the fact that the public purse is now effectively what funds the City's new generation of financial phalli, while the bankers therein squeal against a Tobin tax. That there are worthwhile buildings coming out of this seems beside the point. But even then, nothing has animated the City's malevolence with the demented extravagance of Lloyd's, a building which seemed to scare Rogers and his clients into twenty-five years of worthy sententiousness.

If there's a building which encapsulates in one structure what happened in Britain in the 1980s, and what afflicts it still, then it's Lloyd's of London. Designed by Richard Rogers in 1979, and completed to coincide with the City's 'Big Bang' in 1986, it is usually interpreted in one of two completely inadequate ways. For architectural history, it's a monument to 'High-Tech', a style which arose in the mid-70s as a sort of last flicker from the white heat of the technological revolution, at the hands of currently ennobled, often American-trained architects – Baron

Foster of Thames Bank, Sir Nicholas Grimshaw, Sir Michael Hopkins, Baron Rogers of Riverside. High-tech, or a version of it, has been the dominant form of architecture in the UK for the last two decades, though you can glean a lot from the change in its functions – in the '70s most of the above were designing factories, now, with rare and telling exceptions, they design office blocks, cultural centres and luxury flats with a still residual 'industrial aesthetic'. The other thing the Lloyd's Building is known as is a huge metallic embodiment of the Big Bang, a Thatcherite machine for underwriting in (it features on a Five Star record sleeve, and a shop in the basement still sells Athena-style reproductions of it in moody monochrome). But neither of these two takes gives the slightest indication of how monstrous, compelling and utterly fucked-up Lloyd's is; the architectural critics can't talk about much more than the detailing, the anti-capitalists can't look beyond its (admittedly unpleasant) function. In order to really capture its weirdness you have to go inside. A visit on Open House weekend in September 2011 seemed a good occasion.

One of the many things Lloyd's is about is a strategy of tension between the two complementary factions of the British ruling class. Before Rogers, the insurers were housed in a neoclassical edifice built as late as the 1950s, contemporary with the Seagram Building – an embodiment of a practically unchanging British gentlemanly capitalism, resistant both to modernism and to swanky, brash American finance capitalism. On one level, Lloyd's is 'Wienerization' to the nth degree. It houses one of the oldest institutions of the City of London, an insurance firm dating back to 1688 (neatly contemporary with the 'Glorious Revolution'), and it houses it in the most astonishing futurist structure ever erected in the UK. If it evokes any previously existing buildings of any kind, then they're almost always industrial, or specifically petroleum-linked – oil refineries, or the North Sea Oil Rigs which proliferated off the east coast of Scotland in the 1970s, much beloved of high-tech architects. Both of these are visually striking typologies because of their sheer utility, because their functional parts are in no way sheathed or hidden, and because the refining process requires the baffling, twisting intricacies of pipes and gantries. Like so many things with Lloyd's, you can just tick off the political-economic resonances – the oil boom that kept Thatcherism secure in its confrontations with the unions providing inadvertent inspiration for the aesthetic of the City itself at the exact point it was let off the leash.

Maybe this was some kind of unacknowledged appeasement of the gods of industry, paying tribute to it at the same time it was being destroyed. It's also possible that Lloyd's was and is especially thrilling for people who have never worked in a factory, the only other kind of place where services, pipes and ducts are habitually left so bare, since 'nobody' is looking. Maybe. If there is a specific non-industrial built precedent, though, it's Rogers' earlier Pompidou Centre, the first of a very long and still unbroken line of non-specific cultural centres and tourist draws with wilfully spectacular architecture erected across Western cities. The 'Beaubourg' is often considered to be a '6os dream come true: Joan Littlewood and Cedric Price's adaptable, anti-architectural 'Fun Palace', completed and then named after an anti-*soixante-huitard* Gaullist. The '68ers immediately moved to disavow it, of course – the fantasy fiction *The So-Called Utopia of the Centre Beauborg* was the gauche's 'don't give me what I want' response – but if it looks like a Fun Palace, quacks like a Fun Palace, etc. … You can see where I'm going with this. An industrial aesthetic is used for Fun and then is used for Capital. The finance-entertainment complex.

What makes visiting Lloyd's such a bizarre experience, however, is seeing how the underwriters have conserved so many elements of their atavistic previous existence. These remnants are scattered around the new building, decontextualized fragments ripped from 1763, 1799, 1925 and 1958, rudely riveted onto the ducts and pipes. There's the antiquated uniforms worn by the service staff; the front façade of the 1920s offices is held up like a trophy on street level; inside, the Lutine Bell sits at the foot of 'The Room', more of which later; several paintings and bits of furnishings survive from previous buildings; and strangest of all, a complete eighteenth-century dining room by Robert Adam was preserved and recreated. At first, it seems like these are tokens kept on a sort of reservation of gentlemanly capitalism in order to placate the old guard. After a while you realize that what is really happening here is more like a marriage, a reconciliation, a refutation of Martin Wiener's notion of a difference or hostility between the capitalism of gentlemen and the capitalism of industrialists. It happens especially forcefully in The Room.

Agata mentions *Koyaanisqatsi* the first time she sees The Room, and it does closely resemble that film's sense of controlled, mechanized mania. It's an enormous, multi-storey concrete atrium dominated visually by two things, on an axis so that the link between the two is unavoidable. There is a web of criss-crossing escalators, which can take the client to the underwriter at speed. These align with the open-plan offices on every side, creating a sort of visual simulation of industrial activity. It's hard to remember that nothing is actually being *produced* here, and that the look of some putative industrial hub is quoted purely for the purposes of immaterial, literally speculative, finance. The open floors and the dynamism of the escalators draw the eye straight away to the most sentimental of the assembled, decontextualized objects, the Lutine Bell. What you see is a neoclassical rostrum housing the bell itself, made in the 1920s, all mahogany and Corinthian columns, with an antiquated clock on top. The bell inside is rung when a member of the Royal Family dies, and on the rare occasions when a ship they have insured sinks, as was its original function. After that, look up, and you'll see a glass barrel-vaulted roof. You're in a gigantic 1980s version of The Crystal Palace, the 1851 iron-and-glass fantasia that Wiener considered British industrial capitalism's unsurpassed zenith. These two emotive remnants are what the whole high-tech assemblage revolves around. Like the Gothicism of the services on the façade, the Room is a quite ridiculously thrilling thing to behold; you have to catch your breath and remind yourself where you are. What this is.

With its glazed lifts, moving parts, girders, cranes, components all crammed into a tight, fierce, metallic mesh, the Lloyd's has always exerted (on me, at least) much the same shivers-down-spine effect as 'Strings of Life', or 'Trans-Europe Express': a mechanical sublime that sweeps away any residual humanist resistance with your willing participation. Fully aware of this, the architect has also left us a series of get-out clauses here. Rogers was and is a figure of the soft left; as a Labour Party peer, he may have been one of those who were the NHS's unlikely last line of defence in the House of Lords. The other stylistic influence here, one which Rogers draws attention to in his books, was the unbuilt projects of the early Soviet Union. The lifts shooting up and down the metal frame are taken from the Vesnin brothers' Leningradskaya Pravda project; the overwhelming metal-on-metal rush of the street façade is taken from Iakov Chernikhov; the irregular, techno-Gothic approach to the skyscraper is from Ivan Leonidov. So add to the list of ironies that the era when the USSR was considered to be capitalism's gravedigger is here being evoked, on the eve of its suicide, for the purposes of the forces that would soon drag its territory into gangster capitalism. Another get-out clause is adaptability. The building is adorned at the top by fragments of the cranes used to construct it, as if to tell us that the thing is in flux; the floors, too, are moveable. The suggestion seems to be that one day it could all be made into something else by someone else. The building has just been Grade 1 listed, so that's certainly not happening, pending another glorious revolution. Then there's the promise of an organic, reformed and reformist city, which made Rogers the spokesman for New Labour's laudable but appallingly executed town planning policies, in which capacity he was probably the last major British architect to have any ideas about society whatsoever. From 1997 to 2010 the architect had a semi-governmental role advocating street life, compact cities, let's-be-like-Barcelona-rather-than-Texas. But the Lloyd's Building, no matter how astonishing it might be to look at as a passer-by, meets the street with a moat.

The real moment of madness in Lloyd's is the Adam Room. While much of Lloyd's evokes the more ruthless side of '80s cinema – a John Carpenter film, *The Terminator*, *Robocop* or *Gremlins 2* could all be shot here – this place is pure Tarkovsky. Specifically, it's the last scene of *Solaris*, where the alien intelligence re-creates the familial hearth. On the eleventh floor, the high-tech corridors, with their Gigerish sculptural ceilings, suddenly meet a white concrete block. That concrete block is decorated with classical details. Lloyd's is not generally thought of as postmodernism, in the usual sense of irony and historical montage – in fact it's often presented instead as 'late modernism', a strident keeping-of-the-faith; Rogers' continuing role as antagonist to the Prince of Wales helps that presentation. Yet here's an absolutely pitch-perfect bit of pomo, a seemingly mocking, parodic reproduction of an Augustan eighteenth century thrown into a completely alien context.

Walk into the concrete block, and you're as far into the heart of the establishment as a commoner is ever likely to get (one weekend, every September). The Adam Room, named after its designer, was originally part of Bowood House in Wiltshire, commissioned by the first Earl of Shelburne, and is rammed so full of objets d'art that ten head-bangingly boring series of *Antiques Roadshow* could be built around Michael Aspel inspecting it piece by piece. The sensation it creates is of reaching the inner sanctum of the great parasite itself; all that outside is just for show, a display of how sprightly and modern and with-it we are, a delicate subterfuge, an elaborate joke about deindustrialization where we can look at paintings of galleons while the shipyards are closed. In here, Lloyd's of London are the same organization that grew fat on the slave trade; the room is a time machine that physically brings Old Corruption back to the site of its inception. They play at modernization, but they always keep this place in reserve, are always able to return to it. Inside the Palladian bunker, we circle round the table for our allotted time.

The City's Broken Borders

The Square Mile has always been distinct from the proletarian areas around it, although they are very close in proximity. The markets of Petticoat Lane, Spitalfields and Smithfield, the lawyers and Improved Dwellings for the Labouring Classes in Holborn, the teeming, radical slums of Clerkenwell or Whitechapel, the warehouses of Shoreditch and Hoxton, the interzones just beyond London Bridge in Borough and Bermondsey, all were in recent memory emphatically Not City; the last decade has seen this change radically. The Griffin statues – mythical monsters that guard gold, don't forget – that mark the boundary of the Corporation of London's feudal jurisdiction are a leftover from the 'Ring of Steel' that was put here in response to the IRA's bombing campaign in the early '90s, as are the little observation posts that often adjoin them. The road blocks went a long time ago, but the infrastructure is in place to reassert them at any time, as a day of protest in the City always makes clear. All that security is now part of the City's particular infrastructure, which you could enjoy as being part of some dystopian film had it not become so everyday. The Bloomberg-branded plant pots next to Holborn Viaduct, the little TV screens shaped like dustbins round the corner from the Guildhall … Beyond the Griffins are the areas into which the City has spilled. This shouldn't be overstated; few hedge fund managers are likely to be renting ex-council flats in Aldgate, preferring the old money of Mayfair and Marylebone, and much of the Old Guard surely still makes its way to Reigate or Surbiton at 5.30 pm. Yet enough of it has happened to have had a seismic effect on inner eastern London. This isn't just a matter of extending the offices north and east, as in the munificent, now-mutilated mock-agora of Broadgate, but something more unprecedented – a section of the rich have returned to the metropolitan centre to live, just as all those planning papers said they should. It's the only place where it has really occurred on a large scale, and the result, rather than a jolly knees-up where barrow-boy and banker (as per the pub in Borough) meet on equal terms, is a truly epic class cleansing.

In visual terms the results are not quite what would have been expected. For instance, when the down-at-heel squares, mews and terraces of Notting Hill and Ladbroke Grove were gentrified, they went up in the world aesthetically – newly clean, tidy and scrupulously kept. The City's borders are still squalid in appearance, a chaos of graffiti-caked warehouses, derelict pubs, unlovely estates, ubiquitous rubbish and desperate, often homeless wanderers; the difference is that you now have to be one of the 1 per cent (or a council tenant) to be able to afford living there. The City does not tidy up its edges; it couldn't even if it wanted to, such things being in the hands of the cash-strapped municipalities of Hackney, Camden and Southwark. Sometimes it directly colonizes them, to alarming effect, by simply leaping over the Griffins and parachuting glass and steel into them. This can be seen in Foster's unforgivable emasculation of Spitalfields Market,

Nicholas Grimshaw's blue-glass troll creeping up through Aldgate to Whitechapel, and most obviously, the leap cross-river into Borough, in the form of Piano's Shard. The movement that interests me most, perhaps because it is the stealthiest, is the movement south of the river, across London and Tower Bridge into the City of Southwark.

Across London Bridge, aside from the unavoidable Ryugyong Hotel that now bestrides the railway station, there are subtler signs of the City's colonization. The river, usually a location for prosperous housing, is at first blocked off by the stone-clad '80s offices of 1 London Bridge, so you walk on the main road, past the overhead walkway of a surely soon-to-be-demolished concrete shopping arcade, and then get to the river at Shad Thames. This is, if you can screen from your eyes the souvenir shops and offensively-priced eateries, one of London's great ur-modernist spaces – a dense conglomeration of stark, functionalist brick warehouses with walkways and gantries thrown across them – an incredibly exciting urban set-piece, which Disneyfication cannot quite destroy. Upriver for a few yards, and you're now at a place called More London. More London in what manner, you may ask? More 'witty' public art, perhaps; more glazed office blocks and whimsical landscape features, and definitely more private security, but it's pessimistic to consider these all inherent properties of London. It's an instructive space, because on the face of it, More London avoids all the things that make the City itself desolate. There's a mix of uses – a couple of theatres and some housing close by, rather than solely underwriters, merchant banks, multinationals and such. There is a big 'public' Thameside promenade, although as this is privately-owned space you'd be advised not to do anything naughty on it, like, say, picket the offices of KPMG. The key building however is public, the headquarters of the Greater London Authority. Designed, like most of More London, by Foster & Partners, it follows the Reichstag model of 'transparency' in form and, pretty please, in function also; but it is notable for not being owned by the GLA itself. They have a lease from the developers. Not only did the GLC's County Hall get sold off for a hotel, an aquarium, a *Star Wars* exhibition and 'Dali Universe', but its alleged replacement was not, in the era of the property-owning democracy, allowed to own its own home. The emasculation of local government is complete – the GLA exists on the City's sufferance, not the other way round.

Bermondsey – for that is where we are – is notoriously (and has always been) one of the poorest Zone 1 districts, and one so authentically Cockney that a certain type of writer gets very dewy-eyed here. The housing isn't very proper Cockney, however, and there are few stock-brick terraces left; you have to go as far east as Deptford for the built fabric to really resemble Dickensian London, if that's what you're after. The main road, just off More London, is taken up by the mammoth development of 1890s Peabody Trust tenements that screened slums from the visitors to the new Tower Bridge – on a real metropolitan scale, if not a 'human' one. But follow the riverside and the contrasts get sharper. The housing developments here are alternately carved out of old warehouses or designed anew by enduring '80s postmodernists CZWG. These architects always highlighted the rupture they made with the existing fabric, always signposted their interventions and their lack of historical fidelity. In the middle of these purple and pink housing complexes and fluted, art deco-style devices is a seemingly Corbusian building, small and apparently rational. This is the Design Museum, designed in 1989 by Conran, who remoulded a 1950s stock-brick and concrete warehouse to make it look as much as possible like a white-walled Le Corbusier villa from 1926. In the process, the joins were no longer visible, the historical fiction was hidden; the raw and untutored aesthetic of industry became a good-taste 'industrial aesthetic'. It's one of the most influential buildings of the last couple of decades.

Eventually, this riverside of yuppiedromes is interrupted, at least as a public promenade. But it is continuous: apart from the derelict sheds of Convoys Wharf and later the Thames Barrier, there is an almost unbroken strip of 'stunning developments' stretching along both sides of the river as far as Thamesmead, Barking and beyond; one of the most striking and seldom commented-on changes in London over the last decade. An entire linear city of executive housing now stretches for miles along the Thames, without ever seeming to have been planned or discussed;

there was no consultation, no vote about whether London wanted its formerly working river to become a green glass, red terracotta and aluminium balcony Riviera. Even architecturally, pickings here are slim; the Boroughs have none of the Corporation of London's capacity to dictate quality to developers.

So we fork off the river here, past high-end furniture stores and the empty space where until very recently the decaying deco husk of Chambers Wharf and Cold Storage stood, to the unfortunately named Dickens Estate. This was where the late proleface angel Jade Goody grew up. Architecturally it is undistinguished, a completely standard piece of municipal modernism. At the time, Bermondsey could have had so much more; today, it could have so much less, like its people being 'decanted' into Eltham while their homes are redeveloped into an exciting offer of one- and two-bedroom flats, of which 25 per cent are affordable or shared ownership. Accordingly, the Dickens is worth defending. Tree-filled greens stand in front of stock-brick blocks of four storeys, with a public square at the heart of it. That square, though hardly jumping with energy and optimism, evidently still serves its function. Rosa's Café, corner shops, charity shops, a printers, a hairdresser called Spendloads-Please. It's easy to say it's depressing, but look at the balconies, clearly very well used by the council tenants, and remember the humanism that existed even at this lowest level of public housing. Just on the other side of the arterial road is the Setchell Estate, a late 1970s 'vernacular' effort that provides a convincing pedestrian space, segregated from cars, while aiming for 'warmth' in its deep pitched roofs. Like the Dickens, it's never going to be iconic, but it similarly maintains a working-class outpost. Its low terraces and perimeter blocks, organized around greens and old people's homes survives, for now, as public housing, Right to Buy notwithstanding. It is places like this that are being targeted by the current reforms to Housing Benefit and council tenure; how, ask the letter-writers to the *Metro*, can these people justify living in such a high-rent area? Who do they think they are, living in a council flat round the corner from the Design Museum?

A Walk Along the Highwalks

There are two moments, though, when the City overlaps with the seeming antithesis of the rapacious capitalism it embodies and propagates. One of them is Middlesex Street, or 'Petticoat Lane'. This old centre of the rag trade is still full of public housing, much of it inter-war council flats of three or four storeys. Neither shops nor people are City types in the slightest; wits are sharper, without the aid of cocaine. It's a sudden plunge right into real London, and vies with Poplar for the most vertiginous juxtaposition of rich and poor in Europe. These places were mostly owned by the LCC, now by Tower Hamlets, and hence are often left to rot. The City's own post-war housing projects, however, are still a revelation. It's incredible at this distance to think that the City could have paid for the Petticoat Square Estate, a place which is, unlike some of the City's other housing projects, still largely uncolonized. This estate, an assemblage of taut angles, overhead walkways, brick and concrete geometries and an elegant skyline, shows that the post-war consensus was in some ways a genuine compromise, rather than merely a holding operation on the part of capital – it was once so dominant that it even cowed the Square Mile into conforming, into building low-cost, high-quality housing for its poorer rate-payers. It is hard to say how long this place will last – but the other two major City housing schemes surely have a very secure future indeed.

The best approach to the Barbican and Golden Lane is along the City of London's Highwalk system. This is a survivor of the replanned, post-Blitz city of Patrick Abercrombie and later William Holford, which entailed a continuous system of walkways liberating the pedestrian from the ground. It's hard to work out what the rationale here was, exactly; there are no hills to connect, and aside from the planners' own creations such as Queen Victoria Street, not much in the way of congested arterial roads for the pedestrian to cross, although pre-congestion charge there was certainly abundant and obnoxious traffic. Whatever the reasoning, now it forms part of the City's counter-intuitive, labyrinthine system of circulation, as much an intriguing eccentricity as the alleyways and Inns. Also, given that the Highwalks are not always commercially successful in letting their rentable space, their promenades provide some of the more characterful places in the City, where tailors and launderettes haven't totally been supplanted by Tie Rack and Costa. It's a wonderful place to get yourself deliberately lost on a Sunday, full of architectural curios; Brutalist pavilions, concrete canopies to protect smokers from the rain, unexpected views of the ruins of London Wall. The Museum of London is here, its clipped volumes enlivened recently by a collection of placards from anti-cuts marches (would that they had marched through here). The Highwalks are not fussy about style; their longest section starts just off St Paul's and runs as much into Terry Farrell's postmodernist space-grabber at Alban Gate as it does past Basil Spence's dynamic, futurist law courts. The eventual terminus of these Highwalks is the Barbican.

As municipal housing, the Barbican, designed between the 1950s and the '80s by Chamberlin, Powell and Bon, is a more complicated proposition than Golden Lane or Petticoat Square: never public housing in the strict sense, although certainly not wholly intended as the luxury enclave it is now. The Right to Buy had as drastic an effect here as anywhere else, it's just that the stockbrokers weren't interested in erecting pediments onto their concrete maisonettes. It's hard to know where to begin with it as a piece of town planning. The achievement, though scorned at the end by a guilt-ridden architectural culture that had replaced its modernist dogmas with a far worse traditionalist pessimism, is astonishing. There is no better piece of twentieth-century town planning in the UK, in terms of scope, quality, and sheer architectural power and melodrama. As a monument to belief in the future, the belief that the old certainties don't matter, that we can live in new ways, with a new conception of space, in a new, democratic city space unencumbered by cars, malls, pettiness and ugliness, it is so magnificent that it's hard not to simply applaud. That it should be occupied largely by brokers and cultural bureaucrats is a tragedy, although when the blue plaque brigade get here they can note the former residences of John Smith, Arthur Scargill and Benazir Bhutto. But aside from the sheer pleasure of its Brutalist-baroque grandeur, the Barbican is mainly of use for deflecting every anti-modernist, anti-urban shibboleth going – it's a high-density

arrangement in beefy raw concrete of towers and walkways, without an inch of 'real streets', without an iota of 'defensible space', that is doing very well, thank you. It is the architectural equivalent of the prevalent socialism for the rich.

However, a socialism for the poor that would be worthy of the name was also built here, around the same time, by the same architects, and the gap is at first almost imperceptible. To walk from the Barbican to Golden Lane, you go past the Barbican's YMCA (as Barbican historian David Heathcote points out, imagine planning permission being granted in the contemporary City of London for a tower block of *teenagers*), and then come to Crescent House, along Goswell Lane. This was in fact built before the Barbican, though it uses an identical architectural language of bush-hammered concrete and baroque curves. Pass through its pubs and caffs, under its pilotis, and you're at the first, 1950s stage of Golden Lane, a series of tough but elegant blocks of flats, with delicately considered public spaces in between. The small pond and garden that sits below some of these flats is one of the most quietly romantic spaces in the entire city. Once, things like this were considered ours as of right.

Gentrification has reached here, of course; Golden Lane is a place where some of London's working class plainly manage to live well next door to architects who are paying through the nose for the same flats. Yet, for the moment, this is one of the places in the UK that really shows how we can create alternatives, how we can create a new, better and more egalitarian city. It's unexpected to find it in the City of London, but there it is, hiding in plain sight. In order to come into being it does need the intervention of the state, of planning, of the division of labour, of technology and industry. Some of these are things rejected by the Occupiers so nearby at St Paul's, Broadgate and Finsbury Square, and in that, they were more Thatcher's children than they might think. If there is hope in the City and in the city, it lies in the possible conjunction of these two estates and the camp at St Paul's. Here the latter's direct democracy, their egalitarianism and anti-capitalism might lose its off-grid, anti-industrial narcissism, and discover the existence, even now, just about, of a fragment of the socialist, egalitarian, modernist city. That encounter needs to happen, and it needs to happen urgently. It is potentially where the future of British architecture and urbanism lies, if it is not to remain the exterior decoration of evil.

Acknowledgements

All drawn frontispieces are by Laura Oldfield Ford. All photographs are the author's except 7.3 by Agata Pyzik. I'm grateful to the following for their sterling help as interlocutors when writing this book, either/both on the ground or online. For several different locations and reasons, thank you to Laura Oldfield Ford, Golau Glau, Douglas Murphy, Robert Doyle, Matt Tempest, Matthew Whitfield, Pippa Goldfinger, Ian Martin, Hugh Pearman, Charles Holland, Joel Anderson (with apologies), Frances Hatherley, Dominic Fox and Colin Ferguson. Adrian Jones and Chris Matthews' blog Jones the Planner (jonestheplanner.co.uk) was a constant source of inspiration and competition. I owe the phrase 'Wienerization' to Robin Carmody. In and about specific places: Michel Chevalier provided the dirt on HafenCity, Roger Steer gave civic counsel in Gravesend, Andrew Stevens dispensed rueful Teesside info. Tony McGuirk, Milena Grenfell-Baines and John Gravell were remarkably tolerant in Preston, Carl Neville had memories of countercultural Barrow, and Rob Annable gave generosity and time in the West Midlands. In Bristol, James Dixon was a fine guide to the walkways and alleys of Lewin's Mead and a great deal else; Petra Davis gave information, James Hatherley and Robert Barry accommodation (with very belated thanks) in Brighton. In Plymouth, Krzysztof and Kasia Nawratek were welcoming hosts, while Robin Maddock and Jeremy Gould gave lived-in detail; Alex Niven had the swipe-card in, and Will Wiles reminisces of, Oxford; Ian Waites organised the trip around the Ermine Estate in Lincoln; Richard King provided car, company and arcadian rural accommodation in the Valleys; Carsten Hermann put us up in Morningside and Miles Glendinning provided municipal food for thought in Edinburgh; Neil Gray, Leigh French and others at the Free Hetherington provided stridently expressed information and analysis in Glasgow; Sophie Kullmann granted invaluable Pevsner assistance for Wales, Edinburgh and elsewhere; Declan Long, Mark Hackett and especially Daniel Jewesbury helped me make some sense of Belfast. Thanks also to those I may have forgotten. At Verso, Tom Penn, Dan Hind, Ismail, Sarah Shin and Rowan Wilson were all very helpful indeed in taking these from scattered essays into a book. Ellis Woodman and Amanda Baillieu have especially abundant gratitude for re-commissioning Urban Trawl and sticking by it, even after the angry letters stopped. Agata Pyzik remained both patient and animated through all the lengthy train journeys, absences and strains that went into this book. If it is for anyone in particular, it is for her.

Woolwich, March 2012

Notes

1 For reasons of already overstuffed space, I can't say as much here about this impressive building as I would like; I deal with it at considerable length in 'Zaha Hadid and the Neoliberal Avant-Garde', *Mute*, 2011.

2 The MP in question is Nicholas Boles. Toby Helm and Richard Rogers, 'Tory MP calls for local government planning to be replaced by "chaos"', *Guardian*, 18 December 2010

3 The first of these took precedence in both the campaign's slogans and the campaign itself, but was usually shortened, inaccurately, to 'anti-fees protests', when the abolition of EMA and the 80 per cent cuts to Humanities funding were every bit as much an issue, albeit less easy to present as the whining of overprivileged middle class youth.

4 James Meek, 'In Broadway Market', at http://www.lrb.co.uk/blog/2011/08/09/james-meek/in-broadway-market/.

5 The North, that is, as defined by Sheffield-based geographer Danny Dorling, in his essential *So You Think You Know About Britain?* (London, 2011) – a line that begins just below the West Midlands conurbation and Nottinghamshire, and then sweeps down to encompass all of Wales. It is, he claims, the starkest divide in Europe, sharper in terms of wealth and quality of life than North and South Italy or East and West Germany. The problem with Dorling's definition is that, while broadly convincing, it has to be adapted on close examination into a West Bank-style mass of enclaves and exclaves; Tower Hamlets, Chatham or Plymouth have to become colonies of the North, York, Durham and Edinburgh exclaves of the South.

6 See *A Guide to the New Ruins*, passim.

7 Peter C. Baker, 'Eric's World', thenational.ae, 1 May 2008.

8 The income required to purchase an 'affordable' home in London is usually over £20,000 a year; that disqualifies most of the residents of Robin Hood Gardens. Even more drastically, the coalition government's definition of

'affordable' is 80% of market rent, which definitively disqualifies nearly all council tenants.

9 Will Hurst, 'New Robin Hood Gardens Residents' Survey Challenges Demolition', *Building Design* 26 June 2009.

10 In Nowa Huta, the Polish steeltown which Mittal bought up and downsized post-1989, artists put up airbrushed portraits of Mittal on the sides of buildings, on the spaces that Communist Party leaders would once have occupied. It's more apt.

11 A phrase taken from an internal Tory policy agenda briefing, proudly uncovered and publicized by Neanderthal conservative blogger Guido Fawkes at order-order.com, 6 December 2010.

12 See IWCA's 'FAQ' at: iwca.info.

13 My information here comes from an article in *Leopard* magazine, 'Aberdeen's Tower Blocks', by Mark Chalmers. See leopardmag.co.uk/feats, May 2009.

14 See Andrea Klettner, 'Diller Scofidio & Renfro triumphs in Aberdeen City Park competition', *Building Design*, bdonline.co.uk/news, 16 January 2012.

15 Or, at least, for the town planning competence of local government's elected functionaries.

16 Quoted in Gordon Murray, 'Appreciating Cumbernauld', *Architectural Design* 76/1, Profile 179 (2006).

17 This is in fact the clock from the demolished St Enoch Station in Glasgow; taken here under Copcutt and proudly displayed in *Gregory's Girl*, it was attached to its current nondescript corner when the Antonine Centre was built.

18 My guide made a short film about the graffito, in which the 'significance of this text is never explained but it is, in essence, the same story that is told about similar plots of land in every city: a story of dispossession, exclusion, privatization and clearance.' See danieljewesbury.org/gilligan.html and 'Opposition to Barry Gilligan apartments', bbc.co.uk/news/uk-northern-ireland, 18 July 2011.

19 Martin Pawley, 'From Modernism to Terrorism', in *Terminal Architecture* (London: Reaktion, 1997), p. 152.

General Index

Index of Places